STRONG FOUNDATIONS

TWELVE PRINCIPLES FOR EFFECTIVE GENERAL EDUCATION PROGRAMS

Prepared by Participants in the
Project on Strong Foundations
for General Education

THE ASSOCIATION OF AMERICAN COLLEGES
1994

THIS WORK WAS SUPPORTED BY
THE LILLY ENDOWMENT

Published by
Association of American Colleges
1818 R Street, N.W.
Washington, DC 20009

Copyright 1994

ISBN 0-911696-62-8
Library of Congress Catalog Card No. 94-70000

CONTENTS

THE REVIVAL OF GENERAL EDUCATION

JERRY G. GAFF
VICE PRESIDENT AND DIRECTOR
PROJECT ON STRONG FOUNDATIONS FOR GENERAL EDUCATION
ASSOCIATION OF AMERICAN COLLEGES

A broad general education for undergraduate students is an ideal that has guided American colleges and universities since their inception. The earliest colleges offered a uniform classical education, and that tradition continued until the late nineteenth and early twentieth centuries. The growth of science, the expansion and subdivision of knowledge, the development of academic disciplines, and the need for specialized workers—these and other factors cracked the uniformity and gave rise to depth of study in a specialization as a different ideal. Since then, the ideals of breadth and depth, together, have been regarded as the defining elements of quality in baccalaureate education.

In his study of the history of the undergraduate curriculum, Frederick Rudolph analyzed the tension between these competing ideals. He concluded (1977, 253):

> Concentration was the bread and butter of the vast majority of professors, the style they knew and approved, the measure of departmental strength and popularity. Breadth, distribution, and general education were the hobby horses of new presidents, ambitious deans, and well-meaning humanists of the sort who were elected to curriculum committees as a gesture of token support for the idea of liberal learning. When that gesture collided with the interests of the department and the major field, only occasionally did the general prevail over the special.

Because colleges and universities are organized around academic disciplines and departments, including professional and career fields, these special interests tend to overshadow the general education of students.

That is why, for the third time this century, we are again experiencing a revival of general education. As after World Wars I and II, the purpose of today's revival is to assure that all students, regardless of academic major or intended career, receive a broad general education rooted in the liberal arts and sciences.

The term "general education" used throughout this monograph admits of no simple—or single—definition. A heuristic one offered by an earlier report (Task Group on General Education, 1988, 1) is "the knowledge, skills, and attitudes that all of us use and live by during most of our lives—whether as parents, citizens, lovers, travelers, participants in the arts, leaders, volunteers, or good Samaritans." While avoiding advocacy of any particular content, this definition has the advantage of inviting individuals into a conversation, so that a group, such as a college faculty, can determine what are the essential knowledge, skills, and attitudes for students to acquire. If agreement can be reached, then the group can assess the adequacy of a curriculum to cultivate such qualities, or devise a curriculum that would more intentionally nurture those attributes.

Such a conversation about the ends of education takes place today in a climate of serious public concern about the quality of education. The concern centers on the curriculum—at least at the college level—because the debate focuses on what students should know. The concern is not primarily about students being competent specialists in biology, philosophy, or sociology, for instance. It is that students do not possess the marks of a generally educated person—that is, having such qualities as a broad base of knowledge in history and culture, mathematics and science, the ability to think logically and critically, the capacity to express ideas clearly and cogently, the sensitivities and skills to deal with different kinds of people, sophisticated tastes and interests, and the capability to work independently and collaboratively.

A New Concept

Indeed, a new concept of general education seems to be emerging at a large number of institutions that have analyzed undergraduate education. The old idea equated general education with breadth and, in an institution organized around academic departments, involved a sampling of courses from the broad array of academic disciplines. The method of securing breadth was by means of distribution requirements, and students were typically given a great deal of latitude to choose among alternative courses within broad domains of knowledge, such as the humanities, social, and natural sciences. Usually all courses designated by a department, typically introductory or lower level ones, met the requirements. These courses were regarded as a "foundation" on which specialized study would build. Such a program required little administrative coordination, simply a registrar to verify that requirements were met. Faculty members tended to view teaching such courses as "service" to students who were concentrating in other fields, and students were advised to "get your distribution requirements out of the way, so you can get on with more important work in your major." Each of these elements is part of an old, and increasingly discredited, way of thinking about general education.

A new concept is emerging from conversations among faculties about the qualities of an educated person and the redesign of their curricula. One after another, college faculties are concluding that general education must be much more than breadth and simple exposure to different fields of study. Collectively, they are deciding that students should:

- receive a generous orientation to the intellectual expectations, curricular rationale, and learning resources of the institution;
- acquire specific skills of thought and expression, such as critical thinking and writing, that should be learned "across the curriculum" and imbedded within several courses;
- learn about another culture and the diversity that exists within our own culture in terms of gender, race, ethnic background, class, age, and religion;
- integrate ideas from across disciplines to illuminate interdisciplinary themes, issues, or social problems;
- study some subjects—beyond their majors—at advanced, not just introductory, levels;

- have an opportunity near the end of their course of study to pull together their learning in a senior seminar or project; and
- experience a coherent course of study, one that is more than the sum of its parts.

Surely, study of various disciplines is important, but this increasingly is seen as a minimalist definition that is not sufficiently rigorous for the demands that students will face in their lifetimes. A more robust concept is needed to raise the quality, stature, and frankly, the value of general education.

However defined at an institution—and there is great variation—the new concept is full of educational purposes *beyond* that of breadth. A loose distribution system, which maximizes student choice within broad categories, is inadequate to guarantee that all students acquire this kind of education. Some prescription, whether specific graduation requirements or guidelines for certain kinds of courses (such as "writing intensive"), is necessary. Courses offered by departments must be reviewed by institution-wide committees to assure that they meet specified educational criteria. A great deal of coordination among departments, faculty members, and students is necessary to foster coherence. That is why many institutions with reformed general education curricula create new administrative positions; a director of general education is needed to see that purposes are addressed and coherence is achieved.

Rather than seeing such intentional courses as demeaning "service," faculty members tend to view them as special opportunities to teach the most fundamental ideas, methods, and perspectives of their disciplines to students who may never take another course in the field. Such important courses obviously cannot be "gotten out of the way"; they are essential to the educational enterprise. And a more useful metaphor than a "foundation" is that of a "scaffolding," a structure that exists alongside a major and provides a context and framework for erecting that edifice.

This new concept is a richer, more purposeful, and more demanding concept of general education. Although many of the educational purposes can and should be addressed in academic majors, this new concept gives far more substance and authority to general education.

It demands a better balance with the major.

A Brief History

The current curriculum debate was launched as long ago as 1977 with the confluence of three disparate events. The Carnegie Foundation for the Advancement of Teaching (1977) published a book that declared general education a "disaster area." The U.S. Commissioner of Education and his assistant (Boyer and Kaplan, 1977) called for a common core curriculum as a way to focus on critical issues central to all members of society. And the Task Force on the Core Curriculum (1977) presented Harvard College with a proposal to overhaul its general education program. Each of these events was trumpeted by the media, reinforced each other, and highlighted the need for improvements in the general education curriculum. They kicked off what has become a veritable "movement" to reform general education. By the late 1980s, surveys (El-Khawas, 1987; 1988) reported that virtually all colleges and universities had reviewed their general education programs, and large numbers had made revisions in them.

Three Questions

The movement unfolded in phases that can be sketched by looking at the successive questions that have been raised. *The first question* was, "What is wrong with general education?" Boyer and Levine (1981, 3) declared that "general education is the spare room of academia with no one responsible for its oversight and everyone permitted to use it as he will." They argued that it will never be a "strong and vital part of collegiate study until it has a recognized purpose of its own." William Bennett (1984) and E.D. Hirsch (1987) provided a different type of response by lamenting that many students graduated without studying important areas of learning, resulting in a lack of what the latter called "cultural literacy." The lacks cited by these and others are as diverse as history and literature, science, technology, and mathematics, and writing and computing.

College campuses had their own answers to the question, as can be seen from the sixty diverse institutions that in 1978 applied to participate in a project I was directing, General Education Models. The project was designed to bring together a group of colleges and universities to strengthen their general education curricula. Applicants were asked to describe the problems with their current programs, which were almost entirely loose distribution systems. The group noted five sets of problems.

1. Their curricula lacked an educational philosophy and were based essentially on political compromises.

2. Their programs were fragmented and described as a "smorgasbord" or a "Chinese dinner menu."

3. Students were lacking in interest, motivation, and skills to master traditional liberal arts subject matter and did not see the utility of the material to their careers.

4. The faculty had little interest in teaching non-majors or connecting their content with other fields, and the quality of teaching in general education was a concern.

5. The decentralization of responsibility for general education to twenty, thirty, or forty more or less autonomous departments meant, in the words of one, "no single body [is] responsible for the development, supervision, or evaluation of general education." Of course, this is a perfect prescription for a fragmented curriculum without an educational rationale.

A second question was asked, "What is to be done?" Of course, a wide variety of answers was offered, many in the form of so-called national reports. Speaking on behalf of the National Endowment for the Humanities, Bennett (1984) proposed study in six humanistic fields. The Association of American Colleges (1985) called for the establishment of a "minimum required curriculum" and spelled out nine components. AAC also challenged academic administrators to "revive the responsibility of the faculty *as a whole* for the curriculum *as a whole.*"

The Study Group of the National Institute on Education (1984) recommended that all students should have two full years of liberal education and that more resources should be shifted to the first two years of college. Their major thrust was not toward any particular content but, rather, toward involving students in whatever content they may be studying.

Lynne Cheney (1989) favored distributing fifty semester credit hours of study across several subjects: one semester on the origins of civilization, one year on Western civilization, one semester on American civilization, two one-semester courses on other civilizations, two years of foreign language, one year of mathematics, one year of laboratory science, and one year of social science. AAC's Task Group (1988) analyzed some of the most difficult issues in implementing strong general education programs and made a series of recommendations about planning, teaching, and organizing support for general education. These last two works were filled with institutional examples of good practice, a sign of the progress being made in elevating the idea and practice of general education on the nation's campuses. In the words of the latter:

> We sense lively debate and invigorated practice at those institutions in which faculty are willing to engage in the necessarily prolonged analyses and experimentation in general education courses and programs. (p. 57)

Another question arose, after over a decade of debate and reform: "What are the consequences of the curriculum changes?" This question has not been fully answered, although various reports from individual campuses and a few research studies have been completed. Most of these have focused on curricular components, and the early evidence suggests that:

- Freshman seminars tend to be popular with students and faculty, and they seem to foster higher achievement, greater satisfaction, and better retention rates (Fidler and Hunter, 1989).
- Writing across the curriculum has been one of the most successful and influential themes of reform. It has touched nearly all campuses, as thousands of professors in all fields are teaching writing in their courses.
- Courses and sequences dealing with international cultures and cultural diversity domestically are increasing. After sixty-three institutions developed new courses and instructional materials in the Engaging Cultural Legacies Project, AAC assembled sixty more to work on development of courses dealing with domestic diversity in

its current American Commitments Project. There is
some evidence that such courses help students learn
how to think, talk, and deal interpersonally with issues
of diversity (Musil, 1992).

My own (1991) study of the early outcomes of changes in general
education suggested that they not only led to increased quality and
coherence, but they also had a positive impact on other parts of the
institution. For example, over 65 percent of the institutions reported a
positive impact on the sense of community, the renewal of faculty, and
the identity of the institution. For those which reported making a
large change in the curriculum, over 80 percent cited these benefits.

Obviously, more systematic study is needed regarding the outcomes of curricular changes, but the evidence is starting to document
the benefits of more rigorous study.

The New Question

These first three questions remain very much with us. Indeed, new
analyses of the problems (Anderson, 1992; Carnochan, 1993), new
suggestions for improvement (Schneider, in press), and new reports of
consequences (Tinto, Goodsell-Love, and Russo, 1993) continue to
appear with regularity. Similarly, new institutions commence
curriculum reviews, significant new curricula continue to be approved,
and institutions having made modest changes continue to work for
more substantial change. But, among this ferment of activity, a new
question is pressing for attention.

With large numbers of colleges and universities having made significant investments of time and money to design and implement new
general education programs, they are concerned with maintaining
their momentum. "How to sustain vitality in strong general education
programs?" is a question that is asked by increasing numbers of individuals. Answers to this question are vital if we are to reap the rewards
of the substantial progress that has been made in many institutions.
Without clear answers—and action based on them—today's innova-
tions are in jeopardy. If we go back to business as usual, if we fail to
nurture strong general education programs, we will repeat the same
unfortunate—and wasteful—historical cycle that sees general education wither until another revival is needed.

To answer the question of sustaining vitality, AAC organized the "Project on Strong Foundations for General Education," with support from the Lilly Endowment. From among 116 applicants, seventeen diverse institutions were selected to develop answers to the question. The institutions operated very different general education programs, and while all continued to work on improvements, they were quite eager to sustain the progress (typically quite substantial) that had been made. Campus leaders met periodically for two years to share experiences and insights. The document that follows is a genuinely collaborative writing project that represents the group's best thinking about how to answer the emerging new question.[1]

When we initially thought about writing this report, participants considered describing their own programs, because, collectively, they are at the forefront of the reform movement. They considered highlighting the most distinctive aspects of their curricula and noting variations in approaches taken at different institutions. But they decided against that, partly because these curricula seemed to be institution-specific and not what they, in good conscience, could universally recommend to others.

Eventually they came to believe that those curricular components are not really the most important things to speak about. Rather, they decided that the specific structure and content of their programs were less important than the underlying principles on which they are built. Like the iceberg, program features are visible, but the most fundamental features of strong general education programs are the invisible principles that lurk beneath the surface.

They set for themselves, then, the very ambitious undertaking of ascertaining just what those basic principles really are that make a vibrant program and sustain its vitality. That led to a great deal of collective soul-searching. Everyone had to reflect on their experiences, think hard thoughts, hold cherished beliefs up to criticism, and share their stories—both good and bad—with each other. They critiqued their best ideas, clarified their thinking, and tried again—and again—to express their most basic thoughts.

Eventually the group settled on twelve principles. It is not that there are exactly that many, but that was the number that captured the most important things they agreed on, given the basis of their experiences in seventeen very different institutions and programs. Readers will notice some overlap among the principles, but each represents a way of thinking, or a lever that can be pushed or pulled, to effect institutional change.

Following the path recommended in this volume will almost assuredly require institutional change. This is because, as we have noted, most colleges and universities are not organized to make the general education of undergraduate students a top priority. Starting with the general education curriculum, the group soon saw the need to examine all aspects of the academic culture and organization for ways each office or unit facilitates or impedes learning in the formal curriculum. The admissions office, student advising, the norms of student life, faculty hiring, the reward system, budgeting priorities, fund raising: these and everything else that happens on a campus can provide positive support for general education—or can undercut it.

Of course, this approach means that no single institution can stop nurturing its general education program. No place has reached general education Nirvana; none has a perfect program; each must continue to refine its own program. As soon as institutional attention wanders, the curriculum may start falling apart. It may become less coherent; students may not see the point of certain requirements; required courses may be routinely taught and receive poor evaluations from students.

Also with inattention, parts of the institution may stop providing positive support for the curriculum: admissions officers may revert to simply recruiting bodies rather than explaining institutional expectations and the rationale behind the curriculum; student life may succumb to inherent anti-intellectual tendencies; faculty may be hired with little regard to their teaching of non-majors; the reward structure may discourage faculty members from teaching general education courses; and so on. These are all danger signs.

Our prescription is not an easy one. Hard and persistent work is needed to sustain quality and coherence in a curriculum. As any academic leader knows, getting faculty members to pull together is a bit like herding cats. Good teachers know they face a constant challenge to involve students actively in their own learning. Breaking down bureaucratic walls and corralling the various institutional forces so they can move together to support general education is a constant struggle.

But the virtues of this particular twelve-step program are two: it is brutally honest, and it is most helpful to others seeking to strengthen the general education of students—and to sustain those vital programs. Like other twelve-step programs, this is a form of "tough love" for colleges and universities. If students are to receive a high standard of quality in baccalaureate education that includes *both* a strong general education *and* a specialization, institutions will have to change some of their habits. Both of these ideals can co-exist within the same institutions—but not unless general education is truly valued and strongly supported by institutional policies and practices.

The contributions of all of the individuals involved in preparing the following report—including my own—have been transformed as a result of our involvement in a collective enterprise. Extending thanks to specific people would be both imprecise and inappropriate for such a group effort. Since the beginning, however, participants in the Project on Strong Foundations have been animated by the sense that we were collaborating on an important task. In the end, we created not just an essay but also friendships, mutual respect, refined understanding—in short, a genuine community of scholars. I want to express my profound appreciation to each of my colleagues for all that we were able to create together.

---

[1] A related work focusing on the difficulties of implementing new general education curricula is nearing completion. Kanter, S., London, H. Gamson, Z., Arnold , G., and Civian, J. *Subtexts and Garbage Cans: Reforming General Education* will be published by the New England Resource Center for Higher Education at the University of Massachusetts at Boston later in 1994.

WRITING THIS REPORT

The writing of the present report was a genuine collaborative activity. In some respects, the process of developing this document parallels the development of a strong general education curriculum. That is, it progressed in direct proportion to the development of understanding, trust, purpose, and community among the participants.

The original idea for this report came from Carol Schneider, Executive Vice President at AAC, during the first Project meeting in January, 1991. Recalling AAC's earlier leadership with *Integrity in the College Curriculum* and *A New Vitality in General Education*, she challenged the group to follow these with recommendations for sustaining vitality.

The group was excited by the idea, then seen as a distant possibility. Of more immediate concern was getting to know each other and to learn from the accumulated wisdom in the group. Initially conversations among participants were cautious and laden with an abundance of official institutional rhetoric. Group members focused on the considerable differences among the institutions and their curricula.

When it came time to consider the nature of our report, some argued strongly for a report that would contain seventeen "case studies," highlighting the variety of effective approaches to general education and to sustaining its vitality. Others argued for a report based on what we held in common. They asserted that if we could agree on a set of recommendations, that would make a greater contribution, precisely *because* the group contained so much diversity. Eventually we embarked on the task of writing a coherent document with a single, strong voice. Nobody was convinced that we would succeed, but we resolved at least to try.

We first worked on developing a set of mutually agreed-upon propositions, which we later came to think of as basic principles. Our original list contained eight, and they eventually expanded. As we met and discussed each one, we started to develop a rationale for the group's positions.

The need to move from talking to writing soon came. We assembled a "drafting" committee in order to capture the essence of our discussions and to fill in some of the blanks when the group was silent on certain issues. The drafting committee consisted of Jacqueline

Johnson, John Nichols, Karen Schilling, Christina Sorum, and Sheila Wright. At that time we had ten principles, and five drafters; each person agreed to write some prose about two principles. About the best that could be said of the combined result was that it was a beginning. As might be expected from such a fragmented process, each principle was written in a different style; some discussion was weak; overlapping discussions were apparent; and conflicting perspectives emerged. These and other problems were pointed out at the next project meeting. After a lot of soul-searching, the group decided to stay the course and make another stab at a "coherent document that spoke with a single, strong voice."

This time the drafting committee divided into two teams, each with responsibility for fashioning more coherence in each of two parts. Participants from all seventeen institutions agreed to write short examples and anecdotes that could be used to illustrate the principles. These were incorporated into the next draft. That one was better but still well short of professional standards. More criticisms and suggestions were offered, including a review by members of the Project Advisory Committee.

The final draft was assembled by Karen Schilling during the summer and fall of 1993, drawing on further material submitted by most participants. Bridget Puzon, Academic Editor at AAC, edited the document to give it its current style and flow. Audrey Jones typed and produced each of the several versions of the manuscript.

Like a strong general education curriculum, this document is a better one than could have been produced by any single person. It represents, collectively, more insight and wisdom than the sums of separate parts. It stands for the achievement of a coherent vision by the group over the persistent tendencies toward fragmentation. At last, it represents the considered convictions of a group who were strangers to one another two years ago.

INSTITUTIONS AND PEOPLE

PARTICIPANTS IN THE PROJECT ON STRONG FOUNDATIONS FOR GENERAL EDUCATION

Arizona State University, Tempe, Arizona
    Toni-Marie Montgomery, Associate Dean, College of Fine Arts
    William Johnson, Director, University Evaluations
Ball State University, Muncie, Indiana
    B. Thomas Lowe, Director, General Studies and Academic Programs
The College of St. Scholastica
    Larry Goodwin, Vice President and Dean of Faculty
    Chandra Mehrotra, Dean, Graduate Studies
    Steven Ostrovich, Director of General Education
Grand Valley State University, Allendale, Michigan
    Jacqueline Johnson, General Education Coordinator
    Mary Seeger, Dean, Academic Resources and Special Services
    Barry Castro, Professor of Management
Jackson State University, Jackson, Mississippi
    Inez R. Morris, Associate Professor, English
Miami University, Oxford, Ohio
    Karen Maitland Schilling, University Director of Liberal Education
Minnesota Community Colleges, St. Paul, Minnesota
    Terry Dilley, Professor of Sociology, Austin Community College
Roanoke College, Salem, Virginia
    R. Scott Hardwig, Professor of Fine Arts,
    Susan Millinger, Director of General Education
St. Joseph's College, Rensselaer, Indiana
    John P. Nichols, Core Curriculum Coordinator
San Jose State University, San Jose, California
    Cynthia R. Margolin, Associate Dean, Undergraduate Studies
Southeast Missouri State University, Cape Girardeau, Missouri
    John B. Hinni, Dean, School of University Studies
    Dalton B. Curtis, Jr., Director, Interdisciplinary Program
    Fred T. Janzow, Coordinator, Freshman Year Experience Program

Susquehanna University, Selinsgrove, Pennsylvania
    Jack Holt, Associate Professor, Biology
    Linda McMillin, Assistant Professor, History
Union College, Schenectady, New York
    Christina Sorum, Director, General Education
University of Hartford, West Hartford, Connecticut
    Elizabeth McDaniel, Associate Vice President for Academic Affairs
    Marcia Seabury, Director, All-University Curriculum
    Guy C. Colarulli, Assistant Vice President for Academic Affairs
University of Idaho, Moscow, Idaho
    Kurt O. Olsson, Dean, College of Letters and Science
    Thomas Bitterwolf, Director, Office of Teaching Enhancement
University of Maryland, College Park, Maryland
    Maynard Mack, Associate Dean, Undergraduate Studies
University of Minnesota-Morris, Morris, Minnesota
    Elizabeth Blake, Vice Chancellor, Academic Affairs
    Peter M. Whelan, Assistant Professor, Geology

In addition, several individuals who played important roles in the Project have since taken positions at other institutions. Kathryn Mohrman, formerly Dean of Undergraduate Studies at the University of Maryland is now President of Colorado College. Sheila Wright, previously Director of the All-University Curriculum at the University of Hartford, is currently Vice Provost for Undergraduate Studies at the University of Denver. Mary Ruth Cox was Assistant Dean for Academic Affairs at the University of Minnesota-Morris, and now is Assistant Provost at Hobart and William Smith Colleges.

The Project's Advisory Board assisted with several aspects of the Project. Members are listed below.
    Ann S. Ferren, Interim Provost, American University
    Zelda F. Gamson, Director, New England Resource Center for Higher Education, University of Massachusetts at Boston
    Joseph S. Johnston, Jr., Vice President for Programs, AAC
    Arthur E. Levine, Chairman, Institute for Educational Management, Harvard University
    Carol G. Schneider, Executive Vice President, AAC
    Barbara Leigh Smith, Academic Dean, The Evergreen State College
    Ronald A. Williams, Acting President, Lakewood Community College

INTRODUCTION

In a remarkable burst of energy, many American colleges and universities have examined, debated, and revised their general education programs over the last decade. Much has been written about the need to reform general education and about what well-constructed general education programs should look like, what content they should include, what skills they should cultivate, and how they ought to be taught. It is not our intent to duplicate this work, although we will refer to the best of it from time to time.

This monograph is a guide to campus leaders interested in providing strong institutional foundations for general education programs. Given the enormous investment of time and resources spent in developing new approaches to general education, we are interested in identifying implementation strategies that ensure continuing program strength. At the invitation of the Association of American Colleges, we began with our own experience as practitioners—faculty members and academic administrators—who labor day-to-day in the trenches. We reflected on our experience at seventeen diverse institutions, representing the many dimensions of American higher education, and we attempted to answer three questions about program implementation: (1) What characteristics do successful programs share? (2) What common strategies do they employ to secure their sustained vitality? (3) What common problems do they experience?

In moving toward our answers, we proceed inductively to develop a list of principles and to illustrate them with specific examples. The examples are drawn from our seventeen programs and others with which we are acquainted. In the language of the current "quality" movement, our principles represent benchmarks for gauging program effectiveness and should be applicable to a variety of institutions. We hope that the fruit of this process is a useful framework for any institution to analyze and guide its continuous action to provide an effective, broad general education for all students.

Simply stated, our answer to the questions about strong foundations for general education is contained in one overarching meta-principle:

> **A strong general education program articulates a compelling vision and forms an evolving community based on that vision.**

Twelve interrelated principles explicate what is basic to implementing and sustaining strong general education programs.

PART I

ARTICULATING A COMPELLING VISION FOR GENERAL EDUCATION

Principle #1:
Strong General Education Programs Explicitly Answer the Question, "What Is the *Point* of General Education?"

What is the "ruling idea" or "common aim" which a general education program intends to realize? What is the point of general education at a particular institution? These are the most important questions which we think have to be addressed and answered by academic communities if their general education programs are to be built on strong foundations.

The issue is a philosophical one: general education programs are intellectual projects. They ought to be based on a coherent rationale. For example: How does general education function in the undergraduate program? How is its role different from the role of the major or the role of free electives? What is the relation between general education and the specialized education of the major? What is general education preparing students for? Such questions need to be asked and answered up front in curriculum design and implementation.

The insight which underlies the Strong Foundations project is that the single most important thing that colleges and universities need to do to ensure the long-term viability of their general education reforms is to keep clearly in mind what the point of general education is.

Moreover, our initial concern centers on why we teach whatever we teach, however we teach it. What is the purpose of our general education program and the role of our course within it? Until we know *why* general education is important, we do not clearly know what we should teach or how we should teach it.

The authors of *General Education in a Free Society* (1945), offer a similar observation: just as the courses in a major ought to be related to one another and ought to be ordered in relation to some center, "so should we envisage general education as an organic whole whose parts join in expounding a ruling idea and in serving a common aim" (p. 57). As academic leaders at Harvard University discovered nearly five decades ago, when their faculty colleagues rejected their recommendations, achieving such a state of affairs is as difficult as it is important.

At one institution, general education may be viewed as the "arch major," the place where specialized analyses of the various disciplines are synthesized into some whole. At another, the focus may be on human beings as meaning-makers. In such a context, various disciplines may be seen as offering different perspectives of how humans construct meaning. General education, here, would be at the center of a curriculum where human experience in its totality is examined. Many institutions articulate the point of their general education programs in terms of balance, most often between breadth and depth. At another institution, the point of general education may be to provide a corrective to the "careerism" of many students. John Nichols, Coordinator of the Core Curriculum at St. Joseph's College, states that, "If the major aims mostly to help students 'make a living' then general education is concerned with 'how to make a life' or 'how to make a self worth being.' "

Boyer and Levine (1981) studied the purposes proposed in each of this century's three "revivals" of general education. They found fifty different justifications—some of them contradictory. Yet, they observed that the purposes of general education could be divided roughly into two groups: those that promote social integration and those that combat social disintegration.

In the midst of this most recent "revival," we have come to believe that strong general education programs share some common goals relating to preparation for citizenship in a democratic society. We believe that it is the task of general education to prepare students to:

1. understand and deal constructively with the diversity of the contemporary world, a diversity manifested not only in ideas and ways of knowing but also in populations and cultures;

2. construct a coherent framework for ongoing intellectual, ethical, and aesthetic growth in the presence of such diversity; and

3. develop lifelong competencies such as critical and creative thinking, written and oral communication, quantitative reasoning, and problem solving.

Different institutions appropriately emphasize different aspects of preparation for citizenship in articulating the point of general education. Some would fit the Boyer and Levine typology in emphasizing integration and continuity. Others offer what might be seen as a more radical interpretation of preparation for citizenship focused on self-awareness, self-identity, and change.

At the same time we think that these common purposes of general education programs contribute mightily to the pursuit of a vocation and to the economic competitiveness of the nation. Modern work increasingly is "knowledge intensive." To the extent that general education equips students with a broad base of knowledge, an intellectual framework for dealing with the unknown, and the skills of thought and expression, it promotes the practical side of life in work, home, and community.

We believe that it is difficult to implement successfully a general education program when an institution does not have a vision as an operational guide to its instructional programs. Educational vision prevents what Cohen and March (1974) called "organized anarchy." That is to say, vision provides the basic rationale and driving force for an operational program.

Miami University, a state-assisted institution in Ohio, sees its program as preparing students not only to live in a rapidly changing world, but also to participate actively in its transformation. Extensively studied, debated, and approved by the faculty, Miami's Statement of Principles of Liberal Education (1989, 10) provides the bedrock on which its new university-wide liberal education program rests:

> The diverse educational communities of a comprehensive university have a common interest in liberal learning: it nurtures capabilities for creatively transforming human culture and complements specialized work by enlarging one's personal and vocational pathways. Liberal learning involves thinking critically, understanding contexts, engaging with other learners, reflecting and acting, habits that extend liberal learning through a lifetime to benefit both the individual and society.

Howard University, a historically black institution in Washington, D.C., highlights individual identity in articulating the point of its curriculum, noting: "Sureness about one's identity strengthens one's courage to live and to triumph in a hostile or indifferent world." Its version of preparing students for citizenship states:

> Graduates of the College will need to rewrite many of the premises of that world—probably for some time to come—and will need to join in carrying this understanding from the campus to the community. Today's cultural mainstream has emerged from the confrontations and assimilation of varied peoples; it is not the creation of a single racial or cultural group. In the same way, the future mainstream will be enriched and redirected by today's plurality. By understanding the past and seeing the present through the lenses of their own experiences, the College's graduates can fashion a more just and equitable future for themselves, their people, all people.

Howard's instructional program emphasizes the development of identity, especially among its African-American students.

Strong programs reflect the central educational values and commitments of the institution. Absence of clarity about the point, the inclusion of too many purposes, or too many compromises in the design of programs, make effective implementation difficult. Gaps between the rhetoric of program goals and their implementation are inevitable, but when these gaps are too wide, there is no compelling answer to a question about the point of general education. Clarity of vision at each decision juncture in the implementation of a curriculum increases the chances that a general education program and its courses will remain true to their original intentions over the passage of time. Consistent reiteration of a clear common vision may counter strong centrifugal pressures from programs in majors and professional fields. In a time of serious budgetary constraints as we have today, such clarity contributes to program success.

Principle #2:
Strong General Education Programs
Embody Institutional Mission

This principle speaks to two common problems. First, the traditional missions of many institutions are challenged today by competitive market conditions and by economic pressures. Second, missions often are not expressed explicitly in instructional programs. For example, a general education curriculum consisting of loose distribution requirements—the most common structure—may assure a degree of breadth for students, but it may not reflect the distinctive mission of the institution.

A living and vibrant educational vision must be solidly grounded in an institution's mission—its sense of public purpose, its history and tradition, the character of its students, its geographical setting, or its religious affiliation. When there is uncertainty among faculty members, administrators, and other constituencies regarding mission, the general education curriculum cannot embody a compelling vision. The questions of "Who are we?" and "What is it we must do?" need to be answered before a coherent general education program can be put in place. The answers must be repeatedly restated to sustain vitality in the curriculum.

WHAT'S IN A NAME?

St. Joseph's College and San Jose State University (SJSU) may share a common namesake, but their general education programs serve very different populations of students and are embedded in very different institutional settings with different missions.

SJSU is an urban, public university whose 30,000 students are predominantly commuters, frequently attend part-time, and usually work. No single ethnic group predominates on this campus, with its diverse student body of Euro-American, Asian, Hispanic, and African-American students. Two-thirds of the students transfer from other colleges where they complete more than 75

percent of their state-mandated general education
requirements.

St. Joseph's in rural Rensselaer, Indiana, is a Catholic
liberal arts institution with close to 1100 students, mostly
residential, of traditional college age, and of limited racial
and ethnic diversity.

General education requirements at St. Joseph's are all
incorporated into a forty-five-credit, eight-semester
common Core Curriculum. The semester segments of this
Core are each team-taught by an interdisciplinary group of
faculty, and every one of the segments is required of all
students for graduation. The Core constitutes a genuinely
single program of general education, then, for all students,
and it possesses its own rationale which starts in the first
year, ends with a capstone in the senior year, and moves
from the one to the other in clearly defined steps.

To serve its diverse population and programs, SJSU has
adopted a two-tiered distributive model. More than 150
certified courses meet strict criteria, require significant
writing, and address issues of race, class, and gender where
possible. A thirty-nine-unit foundation includes most
traditional breadth and skills areas and articulates directly
with two statewide transfer programs and individual
courses; but all students, transfers and natives, must
complete an integrated twelve-unit program of advanced,
interdisciplinary, issues-oriented courses in residence. By
giving flexibility in the lower division curriculum and
strictly controlling the upper division requirements, SJSU
makes a unique, coherent contribution to the liberal arts
education of all its graduates, while honoring a wide
variety of previous educational programs.

Paradoxically, the curriculum reform process itself can result in a
sharpening or alteration of the mission, identity, and image of an institution, as constituents ask, "What is *special* about our students, our institu-

tion, our education?" This process of questioning and answering must be repeated for each new generation of faculty and students—and these new faculty and students, in turn, will have an impact on the mission.

Consider the liberal arts colleges which have faced more competitive markets for prospective students as well as increasing costs and rising tuition. Many have drifted from their original missions by creating an array of professional and vocational programs. There is nothing wrong with such programs, and these colleges have moved with surprising speed to respond to perceived market demands. But some of these institutions still use the rhetoric of liberal education in describing their programs when, in fact, most students are in career studies tracks. A strong commitment to general education, even in career fields, could continue to be emphasized, consistent with their original missions, but many have not chosen to do so. The following is an example of one that has.

> The College of St. Scholastica, a private Benedictine institution, located in Duluth, Minnesota, describes integration and balance as the point of its general education program. Here integration and balance grow out of the traditions of the Order of St. Benedict. Each Benedictine community is committed to serving the people in its region and to developing the whole person. With a student body heavily enrolled in professional fields, its program focuses on the integration of skills and content within the liberal arts and sciences as well as the integration of liberal and professional education.

A number of colleges have dramatically expanded their programs to serve an older nontraditional adult population. Again, this appears to be impressive and warranted entrepreneurship, except that some institutions have abandoned their own educational principles in such a move. For example, one well-respected women's college added a successful weekend college, but waived all but one of its requirements, in order to be attractive to the new clientele. Another college developed a truly remarkable new core curriculum for its "traditional" students, but continues to operate a number of "centers" around the state for "nontraditional" students with a radically different set of requirements.

When mission statements only minimally correspond to current programs, they provide minimal guidance in establishing institutional priorities. The consequent uncertainty about institutional character more often than not plays out in the full range of discussions about curriculum. In such contexts, coherent and focused general education programs are rarely found. We know of no strong general education program in an institution that has not seriously engaged the question of distinctive mission.

Other liberal arts colleges are trying to articulate ways in which they are distinctive: a "research college," a "public ivy," an "avowedly Christian college," a "one of the top ten," or a "special campus ethos with small classes, individual attention and sense of community." Such definition has curricular implications. In designating itself as "the personal college," Dowling College on Long Island in New York wished to stake out a place that distinguished its programs from near-neighbor SUNY at Stony Brook. At "the personal college" students don't expect to stand in long lines, sit in large classes, and be unknown to their faculty. The implications for curriculum and pedagogy are quite clear. Hampshire's commitment to inquiry and activism permeate its curriculum, as does Berea's commitment to work as a central component of the daily life of its primarily Appalachian, working-class student body.

Missions have been the focus of public scrutiny and criticism at many state-assisted research universities. Historically they have had a mandate to conduct cutting edge scholarship, to offer graduate education in a wide array of fields, to serve their communities, and to provide baccalaureate education to undergraduate students. At this time, the public is calling for greater emphasis on undergraduate education. Many leading universities confront a real dilemma in responding to this new pressure to give increased attention to undergraduate education, to strengthen general education by raising its place among institutional priorities. During times of constricting resources, to raise one priority means lowering another.

Consider the following examples:
- In the wake of several very substantial budget cuts and a faculty report urging more emphasis on teaching undergraduates, the President of the University of Maryland-College Park, proposed that all entering students enroll

in small freshman seminars. Such a costly new venture, subsequently adopted, was designed to create a particular niche for the University and retain an edge for this flagship institution in competing for the most capable high school graduates from the state.

- Arizona State University, a complex university with 48,000 students, renounced the old pattern that gave curricular autonomy to each of its separate colleges to establish a university-wide General Studies program. To oversee its implementation, it created a University General Studies Council to approve and evaluate courses. Toni-Marie Montgomery, Chair of that Council, declares,

> To have a comprehensive General Studies program at a large research university comprised of thirteen fiercely independent colleges is a triumph in itself. Rather than having a small General Studies core, we have an extensive menu of courses from which students may choose. A narrow core program was simply not politically feasible, and the extensive list of courses has other practical advantages. The impact of the General Studies program on resources was diffused across the university; it was possible to implement the program all at once using existing courses; and almost immediately the program was deeply imbedded in the university curriculum. Moreover, a broad program allows students the flexibility they need to work out complex programs of study involving university, college, and major requirements.

See Appendix A for other examples.

Missions of comprehensive colleges and universities are necessarily complex and multilayered. This complexity often reflects the history of changing roles and character of these institutions. Jackson State University is a classic example. Its mission statement details the history of its development as well as its aspirations for the future: see Appendix B.

Once an institution manages to clarify its mission and devise a vision for its course of study, it needs to make sure that they are carried out not just in the curriculum but also in other key functions. Leadership, strategic planning, faculty appointments, awards ceremonies, budgeting—these are all ways to link mission and vision to a vital general education curriculum.

The University of Idaho has incorporated specific goals and activities for general education in its recently published strategic plan. Idaho's Provost has articulated the need for broadly educated professionals in agriculture, forestry, and other professional fields.

The University of Utah uses the yearly appointment of a Distinguished University Professor to communicate the importance of its General Education Program throughout the institution.

At Ball State University, the Lawhead Teaching Award in General Studies is awarded yearly to acknowledge the work of an outstanding faculty member teaching in General Studies. The award of $1000 carries with it a dinner, a plaque, and recognition at the fall faculty meeting.

Principle #3:
Strong General Education Programs Continuously Strive for Educational Coherence

It is the task of general education to introduce students to the breadth of knowledge and also to the lifelong project of making sense and creating coherence out of the variety. This task involves cultivating the highest of critical thinking skills, what John Henry (Cardinal) Newman (1873) called "the integrative habit of mind."

Undergraduate education often strikes students as a bewildering introduction into diversity: different bodies of knowledge, modes of inquiry, ways of knowing, voices, historical periods, and cultures. This centrifugal exposure to diversity is an essential component of *the point* of general education (Principle #1). And yet an equally essential component of general education is the counterbalancing centripetal pursuit of coherence. Thus, general education *starts* with diversity but *aims* at coherence.

The coherence that counts is that which students and faculty members experience in day-to-day, week-to-week, semester-to-semester, and whole-four-years of general education. All too often students experience the curriculum as fragmented. Separate courses and academic disciplines typically stress particular content and approaches rather than searching for commonalities or making connections between fields. Students are often left adrift in their search for meaning or enlightening connections.

Seeking "the connectedness of things," as Mark Van Doren put it, is a defining goal of strong programs of general education. This deliberate attention to finding and making connections must extend from program design to the many daily details of program implementation.

Coherence: Means to Achieve It

1. Content: One way to pursue coherence is through *content*, and several avenues exist. If all students study exactly the same core courses, as they do at places as diverse as St. John's (Annapolis) and Brooklyn College, they have an opportunity for integration. Although few institutions are willing to structure the entire general education curriculum that tightly, many have what Zelda Gamson calls a "modified core" featuring common learning in the form of a first year seminar, a specified course, or a sequence of courses in the humanities or sciences. In addition to fostering the "integrative habit of mind" within these courses, this approach has another advantage. Instructors in other courses can refer their own work to common material which students study in the core, thus fostering connected learning beyond the core courses.

Interdisciplinary courses represent another approach; they express the interconnectedness of knowledge by presenting multiple perspectives on issues, concepts, texts, or "real world" problems. The All-University Curriculum at the University of Hartford utilizes this approach.

For example, its course entitled "Hunger: Problems of Scarcity and Choice" integrates biology, philosophy, economics, and sociology in a problem-centered focus.

Senior capstone seminars or projects are another means for achieving integration through content of general education.

> At Roanoke College, seniors cap their core experience with an interdisciplinary seminar called 'Senior Symposium.' The course aims to give students an opportunity to integrate materials and skills from the general education program and from their majors as they explore a topic of universal significance. Studying with a faculty member outside their discipline, students are challenged to experience the variety of skills and perspectives that students from different majors bring to a common question. Recent topics have included: Scientific Fact and the Art of Knowing; Who Am I: The Quest for Self; The Quest for Justice; and Prospects for Future Change.

> At The College of St. Scholastica, one criterion for approving a senior seminar topic is that the topic attends explicitly to the integration of liberal education and professional training. 'Ethics in the Professions' or 'Meaningful Work' are examples of such integrative topics.

2. Skills: A second way to foster coherence emphasizes the acquisition of certain *intellectual and communication skills.* For example, nearly all general education programs explicitly recognize the need for students to listen accurately, to speak articulately and persuasively, to read analytically and critically, and to write well. Targeting the development of cognitive skills such as critical thinking, problem-solving, and quantitative reasoning is also frequent.

Achieving coherence through this strategy requires a shared understanding of the specific competence, respect for the various ways a particular skill is expressed in different fields, appreciation of the contributions of various disciplines to skill enhancement, and commitment to a program-wide strategy to achieve enhancement of skills. This is a demanding set of conditions, but any less, and coherence may be lost in its implementation.

> The Freshman Preceptorial, required of all new students at Union College, stresses analytical reading and writing in multiple disciplines. Meeting in sections of no more than fifteen, the students read and discuss a number of significant texts. They write four essays on these texts (which are rewritten after peer or professional consultation) and a final paper. The teachers are drawn from all departments of the college and thus provide an interdisciplinary approach in the creation of the reading list as well as in the discussions at the weekly meetings of the preceptors.

3. Ways of knowing: A third strategy to foster coherence is to draw attention to both the common ground and the differences among various *processes or ways of knowing.*

Epistemological stances embodied in our curricular structure will shape the ways students learn well beyond the confines of the materials for one class or for all of the courses in their undergraduate program. Curricula that emphasize mastery of discrete packages will encourage students to package new materials in similar discrete compartments. Curricula that emphasize interconnections encourage students to see such connections.

A strong general education program must grapple with the question of what will make the ways of knowing hold together. At the very least, it must articulate the differences between disciplines in a way that makes meaningful dialogue across their boundaries possible. This is a significant task not just for students, but for faculty as well. Disciplinary orientations and training rarely prepare faculty for engagement in meaningful dialogue across disciplinary boundaries. Thus, general education, whatever the particular details within it may be, should be built not just upon the recognition of different ways of knowing, but on creative ways of making that diversity work intellectually, educationally, and administratively.

> The general education program at Union College requires each student to complete a four-course cluster in Ancient, European, or American history, literature, and civilization. Two of the courses are history surveys that illuminate the social and political events of the past, two are literature or

civilization courses in the period and area in question. The
General Education Board maintains the coherence of the
clusters by enforcing guidelines which specify that the
literature/civilization courses must 'devote a substantial
portion of their content to the study of texts or artifacts
originating in the period and area covered by the matching
history course.'

General education curricula which provide a context and a framework for critique of work in the discipline allow students to understand
both the power and the limitations of disciplinary perspectives. Distribu-
tional models of general education which highlight disciplinary methodologies as ways of knowing and ask students to examine both the
advantages and the limitations of perspectives from a variety of disciplinary frames, offer promise for achieving coherence in this way. Consistent
with this strategy, *The Liberal Art of Science* from the American Association for the Advancement of Science (1990), provides very useful guidance about the construction of general education courses in the natural
sciences to emphasize science as a way of knowing.

In the contemporary intellectual world, the phrase "different ways
of knowing" has come to connote much more than just distinctions
among various disciplines. These questions, too, are implied: Do
women "know" differently from men? Does one's social class influence
one's views of the world? How are ways of thinking conditioned by
where we live? Are ways of knowing or thinking influenced by ethnic
identity, race, or culture?

At Miami University *all* Foundation courses in its liberal
education program must: 'Explore how ways of knowing,
and related factors (such as gender, class, racial identity,
ethnicity, economic status, regional identity, institutional
traditions, religious commitments, philosophic
perspectives, political objectives, among others) affect the
forms in which the subject matter appears.'

4. Personal Development: As a fourth strategy, general education programs focus on the development of *personal qualities* in students in order to enhance educational coherence.

Interpersonal and valuing skills are needed, since education en-
gages the whole person and includes negotiations with others. Dedica-

tion to intellectual coherence requires open-mindedness and tolerance, both tolerance of the views of other people and also of ambigu-
ity. Integration needs also to be critical, so that the very real conflicts
and contradictions in life (what mathematicians call "surds") are not
masked over by a too easy synthesis. To paraphrase Einstein (who was
talking about "simplifying"), a goal for a student in a strong general
education program is to, "Integrate as much as possible, but no more
than that."

Unfortunately, each of these strategies for achieving coherence
emphasize more of what Johnston, *et al.* (1991) have referred to as the
"supply side" of general education programs than to the "demand
side"—students' own processes of perceiving or making coherence.
Although far too rarely acknowledged, program implementation most
often must begin with where the students are and then attempt to el-
evate their knowledge, skills, and personal qualities.

Attempts to foster coherence must also respond to issues of scale.
One large university, with a large distribution program, implemented a
cognate structure requirement to bring together different disciplines or
related topics in pairs of courses. The complexities of organization and
scheduling were so overwhelming for faculty and students that the requirement was abandoned in favor of single, interdisciplinary,
multicultural courses.

However, as William Perry (1970) and Belenky *et al.* (1986) have
argued so convincingly, it is making commitments in the face of multi-
plicity, in spite of relativism that refuses to simplify and clarify, that represents the uppermost stages of intellectual and ethical development.

Strong general education programs, regardless of institutional size
or complexity, should be designed to assist students to move beyond
sheer relativism toward their own constructive positions. What is to
be studied should be continually examined in a context where students are expected to recognize the value of multiple positions. At the
same time, students should be enabled to develop their own beliefs
and commitments in an environment in which cultural relativity and
moral relativity are neither confused nor conflated.

Principle #4:
Strong General Education Programs Are Self-consciously Value-based and Teach Social Responsibility.

Strong general education programs are self-consciously moral and political in nature. Faculty, themselves engaged, will find ways to involve students in a similar critical, active, and reflective process. The issues of societal responsibility, often charged with emotion and ideology, can factionalize the faculty and isolate the general education program, or can bring faculty together to create positive changes in the culture of the campus. Regardless of the tenor of community reception, we believe the political, moral, ethical, and political dimensions of the general education curriculum are present and unavoidable in program implementation, whether or not explicitly stated. We should, as Gerald Graff (1992) puts it, "Teach the conflicts."

General education is obviously and necessarily based on assumptions—explicit and implicit—about what is important, worthy, and valuable. Some courses are included in the required curriculum, others are not. Strong general education programs work to dispel the mystery about such selections.

> One of the objectives of the core curriculum at Susquehanna University is to concentrate on 'educating citizens of the world.' A Core Curriculum Handbook (n.d., 3) introducing the curriculum to faculty and students states:
>
> > The Core stresses what it means to be a member of the human community today. The Core curriculum poses these key questions on behalf of students:
> >
> > > What personal activities and skills are necessary or useful in coping with the immediate learning experience and for continuing the process of learning in later life?
> > >
> > > What habits of thought and expression are necessary to exercise discernment and persuasiveness in controlling the issues of a complex world?
> > >
> > > What philosophical/religious assumptions lie at the foundation of human experience, both individual and collective?

What historical forces, national and
international, have created the present world order?

How do and can the arts enrich the human
experience and enhance human understanding?

What social institutions and factors influence our
individual and collective lives?

What scientific paradigms determine how we
understand the universe, and what scientific and
technological issues affect the quality of human life
on this planet?

What alternative futures are possible/probable for
us, and how will our individual and collective choices
affect the future?

Beyond detailing such sets of explicit questions related to program
objectives, designers and implementers of strong general education
programs must also pay attention to the silent language of their programs, including that expressed through pedagogies and modes of
evaluating student performance, to ensure that what the faculty collectively value and envision is embodied and highlighted.

Furthermore, strong general education programs are constructed
and designed in such a way that this process of valuing is acknowledged as part of what defines the program itself, and is, in fact, em-
ployed as a device in relation to teaching. Students need to encounter
texts and faculty who are willing to take a stand, to go out on a limb;
students should themselves gain experience in this endeavor. Students
would be better off knowing that a curriculum is something that is
given life in negotiated settlements which are sometimes passionately
achieved; that it is a product of discussion and struggle.

Students must, themselves, have opportunities to be similarly engaged in these reflective, critical, and intellectual struggles, not as ex-
ercises conducted for the purpose of achieving a grade, but as ways of
modeling and practicing active citizenship and individual responsibility to the collective community.

At Grand Valley State University in Michigan a course on
diversity in the United States, developed over a period of
several years in a collaborative interdisciplinary effort, calls
for students in various sections to come together several

times during the semester for plenary sessions. In these
sessions, faculty themselves demonstrate their own
struggles with particular issues and model for students the
ways in which a community of scholars can in fact offer
insight and understanding into complex issues.

As part of their mission, then, general education programs have a
common responsibility to confront multiple problems of the modern
world in such a way that students complete our programs prepared not
only in their disciplines and professions but also in their abilities to
imagine and to construct better—more humane, just, and equitable—
futures for themselves and for others.

The culminating experience of the core curriculum at
Susquehanna University is a Futures Seminar. In multiple
sections, ranging from Managing Tomorrow's Crises, to
World Order Models, to The Future of the World Oceans,
students examine the various methods by which we come
to anticipate alternative views of the future; learn how
beliefs about the future influence current decisions, choices
and actions; and engage at a higher level (than in an
earlier course on values) in a discussion of values, this time
more centered on evaluation and judgment.

The designers of general education programs must include content
and teaching/learning methods which encourage engagement, reflection, and criticism, and which move students away from the uncritical
reproduction of existing patterns of social relations and cultural values.

Strong general education programs provide a rich variety of ways
for students to consider the question "How should we live?" and then
to find ways to encourage and prepare students actually to live their
lives in such a way that their answers to the question are embodied in
their actions.

A document on revitalizing liberal arts education at Howard University states:

The College expects its students to take personal responsibility for shaping the ethical vision that will guide the surrounding worlds. The necessity of choosing, consciously or

unconsciously, means that students need standards for deliberate judgment, some guiding vision of the good. The
College encourages the quest for individual fulfillment in
the context of firm responsibility to those peoples inhabit-
ing the concentric, circling communities—Howard University, the nation, all nations. It aspires to have its
graduates fully comprehend that ethics cannot be separated
from knowledge.

At a Catholic institution like Ohio Dominican the vision of
"How should we live?" that informs their general education program
differs radically from the vision at Earlham, a Quaker institution.
These visions also differ markedly from that articulated at San Jose
State University: see Appendix C.

This charge to educate for responsible citizenship in a world that
is culturally and intellectually complex cannot be taken lightly or
treated superficially by faculties who are engaged in the construction
or implementation of general education programs. The current movement to revise, re-center, or de-center curricula in such a way that the
issues of parochialism and univocality are addressed and in such a way
that cultural pluralism is explored has uncovered a raw spot in the collective life of the faculty. The curriculum debates about culture and
cultural legacy in fact mimic the undercurrent of fear, anxiety, and
hostility which is currently characteristic of the culture's attempt to
address who "we" are and how/whether we can live together in a context which embraces diversity in unity.

Negotiating one's affinities and commitments to diverse
communities within U.S. society is a challenge for all citizens—and a special challenge for liberal education. Cross-
ing borders and boundaries, working cross-culturally,
negotiating difference, sustaining multiple and perhaps
competing commitments, developing one's value scheme
while honoring that of others, making consequential
choices while recognizing significant disagreement, sustain-

ing a sense of relation to the entire polity: These are some of the societal requirements confronting curricula engaging cultural pluralism in America. (*Schneider and Schmitz*, 1992, 111).

Strong general education programs must be implemented in ways that reveal rather than bury the dimension of cultural diversity and other important intellectual, moral, and political struggles in the culture and in the university of the late twentieth century.

Principle #5:
Strong General Education Programs Attend Carefully to Student Experience

Strong general education programs recognize the histories and dispositions of entering students and intentionally play a role in shaping students' experiences at the institution. As Erickson and Strommer (1991) noted, the average faculty member's own freshman year experience is over thirty years in the past. They quote Aubrey Forrest's observations on factors that altered the course of higher education and changed the nature of the freshman classroom. Those who design and teach within general education programs have to contend with the chasm that divides student experiences and the experiences of faculty members ten, twenty, or thirty years earlier. Forrest notes the dramatic impact of the changes during the time between the 1950s and 1980s:

- Enrollment in higher education increased 400 percent to the present 12 million students.
- The number of eighteen-year-olds nearly doubled.
- The high school graduation rate increased from 50 to 75 percent.
- The proportion of high school graduates going on to college increased from 25 to 60 percent.
- The proportion of college students older than twenty-five increased from 20 to 40 percent.

- The proportion of women students increased from 34 to 54 percent.
- The proportion of freshmen enrolled in at least one remedial course went from near zero to 35 percent.
- The proportion of freshmen who had enrolled in at least one college credit course while still in high school went from near zero to 13 percent.
- The proportion of freshmen who delayed entry into college from high school grew from a small percentage to 33 percent.
- The proportion of all college students attending college part-time grew from 23 to 42 percent.
- The percentage of freshmen who expected to work at least part-time while in college grew from a small percentage to 40 percent.
- The proportion of bachelor's degree recipients who took more than four years to complete a degree rose from 30 to 55 percent.
- The proportion of college students who would be characterized as full-time fell from a majority position to 17 percent.

Faculty often know little about student lives today. Student resistance to learning (that faculty often sense) may not be simple negativism, but may represent an expression by students that the classroom is not related to their lives.

Research on who students are and how they learn has never been greater than it is now. Educational researchers and practitioners alike have urged greater attention to student experience: the work of Peter Elbow (1990) and others who study writing instruction, of James Moffatt (1989) and others who observe student culture, of Sheila Tobias' (1990) studies of instruction in science courses, and Uri Treisman's (1985) studies of enhancing the experience of minority students in college mathematics classes. Zelda Gamson (1985) has persuasively argued that strong general education programs begin and end with student experience: tailoring both curricular and co-curricular experiences to engage and empower students as active learners, and recognizing the diversity of needs and strengths that students bring with them.

There is rich variety in First-Year Experiences programs piloted at the University of South Carolina by John Gardner, in specially designed first-year seminars at institutions as varied as Massachusetts Institute of Technology and Southeast Missouri State University, and in the Mentoring Project at the University of Denver. These are ways institutions attempt to foster interchange with students and to allow faculty to know students. At the same time, students gain knowledge of the faculty and of the institution.

The first quarter seminar course at the University of Minnesota-Morris, called Inquiry, consists of weekly convocations with noted scholars lecturing on a variety of multicultural, interdisciplinary topics and two related group discussion sessions per week with fifteen or fewer students. The goals of this first year course are:

- to make explicit how the intellectual life works;
- to emphasize the need for shared knowledge, both historical and contemporary, through reading and discussion;
- to teach the relative importance of good questions over "right" answers;
- to expose the indeterminate and fluid nature of the intellectual process;
- to encourage the development of sound values translatable into positive actions;
- in short, to help students discover how to learn and how to make informed judgments.

The required first year seminar at Southeast Missouri State University, entitled "Creative and Critical Thinking," introduces students to the general education program, available instructional resources, the value of a liberal education, and the dispositions and skills they must develop to become effective thinkers.

See Appendix D for Grand Valley State University model.

Strong general education programs provide supports for helping faculty and staff also cross the divides between "us" and "them," so that in the best of circumstances students are met halfway. These programs draw on a rich variety of involving pedagogies to cultivate and exploit student experience, rather than denigrating or belittling those experiences. Such programs work to untangle the sources of student resistance, rather than to ignore them. In strong general education programs there is an acknowledgment that much of liberal learning occurs outside the classroom and in spite of formal curricula.

In attending to student experience, general education programs find ways to invite students into an educational process that has the potential to transform their personal lives. Faculty in such programs are required to move—in awareness and attentiveness if not literally—into the complexity of the world students inhabit and into recognition of students' diversity. Through this process, faculty develop insight and a reflective, critical perspective into their own experiences as learners "past" and as teacher/learners in the present.

When their ideas, attitudes, perceptions, view of themselves and of the world are taken seriously, students are enabled to connect the curriculum of their lives to the curriculum of the classroom. Students bring their own unique frames of reference, points of view, and resources to the classroom, to ideas, and to texts. Paying attention to student experiences means meeting students where they are and helping them find new perspectives on their lives in the curriculum.

> At Ursuline College, a small Catholic women's college in Cleveland, Ohio, the Core curriculum is built upon an explicit model of student development that mirrors Belenky, *et al.*'s, *Women's Ways of Knowing*. General education courses are designed to facilitate students' epistemological development from the subjective knowing characterizing most entry level students to modes of constructed knowing.

What do we need to know about students and their experiences in order to make general education meaningful to them? We need to know which pieces of the general education program "fit" which students. We need to understand who feels included, excluded or marginalized. We need to understand how and in what way the curriculum and the approaches to the curriculum change students' perceptions of themselves and their world. And we need to know if the changes observed are the ones desired.

At the University of Hartford, the University of Kansas, American University, and Temple University focus groups with students have been used to understand student experiences and their perceptions of general education programs. At Hartford, for example, students' struggles with interdisciplinary courses were illuminated through this approach.

At Southeast Missouri State University, San Jose State University, and at Miami University, students are asked to evaluate the effectiveness of the course in meeting stated program objectives. Both interesting consistencies as well as discrepancies are noted between what the faculty think they teach and what students say they learn.

By attending carefully to student experience, strong general education programs can be designed to close the inevitable gap between faculty intentions and student experiences.

Principle #6:
Strong General Education Programs Are Consciously Designed So That They Will Continue To Evolve.

General education is best seen not as a finished product, but a continuing intellectual and organizational project. On all campuses, curricula are developed in response not only to the more eternal elements of education but also in response to specific circumstances. The existing faculty, the available pool of students, physical resources, and financial contingencies create pressures on the curriculum. In other words, a general education curriculum is not static; it is shaped by creative tensions—and, as such, remains subject to oscillations in the forces of the culture and institutions within which it exists.

Programs must not just be able to change but, in fact, should expect and welcome change. Furthermore, strong programs institutionalize the possibility of change.

The description of the core prepared for faculty and students at Susquehanna University states (p.4): Central to the Core vision adopted by the Susquehanna faculty is the assumption that the Core will evolve constantly: individual courses will change, and the Core as a whole will take on new dimensions as it adapts to a changing world. At the same time, its efficiency and effectiveness depend upon a common understanding of its organization and structure.

A general education program is both *an invention*—a set of courses approved by the faculty, required of its students, and described on a particular page of the college catalog—and something that is in the process of *being invented* by the ever-changing faculty and students who regularly recreate it. The manifestations of this curriculum necessarily assume the most concrete of forms—arrangements of hours, courses, and syllabi within the carefully delineated set of requirements that comprise a college education.

Likewise, when actual courses, rather than abstract titles, fill categories in the curriculum, modifications of these courses or new submissions may result in changed understandings of the original purposes of the curriculum. For example, in moves toward integrating international perspectives into all of the general education curriculum, distinctive categories of world geography related to these issues may no longer serve their original purposes. On many campuses definitions of "Western" and "non-Western" requirements have changed to accommodate new courses on Native American cultures and American ethnic studies. Proposed new courses may challenge the adequacy of our categories for capturing the complexity of our curricula. In other words, general education programs evolve through use.

Strong general education programs recognize and exploit the tension between the invention that was designed and the people who implement the design. Strong foundations for general education are created when program designers build flexibility and strategies of invention within the program's fixed structure.

One of the distinct features of Grand Valley State University's general education program is its peer review process. This process allows faculty to build and sustain program coherence through a cycle of peer discussions in relation to each of the seven categories of their general education curriculum. Faculty who teach in a certain category come together to discuss its goals and objectives, the similarities between the courses which comprise the category, the contribution in general which the category makes to the program, and the strategies, texts, and assignments that each faculty member uses to accomplish the category objectives.

The process of peer review provides a forum for cross-disciplinary conversation, since all of Grand Valley's general education categories include more than one discipline in their offerings. And it provides an informal means of socializing and resocializing faculty into the purposes of the program. The process of peer review also provides an ongoing forum for community—and also for conflict and disagreement inherent in complex communities. Finally, the process allows the vision of the program to continue to be revisited by old and new faculty members on a regular basis.

The evolution of general education programs emerges in the conversation between the leadership of the general education program and the individual faculty who create and teach the courses. In commentary about course submissions as well as decisions about approval and rejection, the program is shaped and reshaped. Through formative evaluations or regularized review processes, individual courses as well as shared understandings of requirements "evolve." Strong general education programs develop mechanisms for moving these "private" discussions of courses and curricula into the regular public discourse of the institution so that program praxis informs program theory.

The science requirement in the general education program at Union College developed in response to what many of the faculty perceived to be a weak requirement in science for the non-science students in the former distribution requirement. Over the years, science and technology courses designed especially for the non-science students had proliferated. These were frequently seen by the faculty and the students as "an easy way out." The General Education Program instituted what is, in effect, a three course mathematics-science requirement in which the science courses must have labs or count for the major and the mathematics course must be taught in the mathematics department (thus excluding any quantitative courses in philosophy or the social sciences). The intent was that science courses be "basic science." As the curriculum has matured, however, it has become clear that the sequencing necessary in "science for scientists" courses may not make them the most useful or appropriate courses for non-science students. Consequently, the general education board has spent a great deal of time reexamining its original premise—that all students should study the same introductory science—and has come to the conclusion that "topic" courses ("The Chemistry of Things," the science of common things; "Seeing the Light: Concepts of Vision" taught by a biologist and physicist; or "World Agriculture" taught by two biologists) may in fact be the better vehicles with which to accomplish their goals. This evolution has been a slow process as new courses were proposed and approved.

Since many of the faculty who implement curricula often are not the same faculty who engaged in the prolonged discussions leading to the original formulation of the models, we must ensure that faculty who are new to our institutions have at least a basic understanding of the intentions of the curriculum and its rationale to participate in ongoing discussions. Without attention to generating this shared consciousness, institutions will likely begin anew the process of curriculum revision when the number of faculty who were not at the institution at the point when the curriculum was first adopted exceeds the number who participated in the process.

In response to a growing need among the faculty to rediscover the idea and design of courses taught in its institutional core curriculum, the University of Idaho created an informal discussion group for faculty teaching in the core. In weekly "discovery" meetings, the faculty reacquainted each other with the program's current offerings. This forum, freed of bureaucratic regimen and busywork, allowed the more than seventy participants not only to examine the intellectual content of existing courses, but to rethink the very culture of the core. The group has generated new core models that would provide sequencing and a greater integration of courses, and now, in subgroups, the faculty are developing new courses to replace old ones. In these deliberations, they have involved campus visitors whose expertise includes the design of undergraduate curricula. Members of the University Committee for General Education have also been invited to these meetings; many have attended, and they will not be surprised, therefore, by proposals that are eventually forwarded from this group. The informality of the discussions has been their strength; while it is critical to retain the university's formal committee procedures for approving courses and academic programs, the "discovery" group can do what formal committees cannot: explore questions of core teaching and learning at leisure and in depth. Taking on the character of a debating society, with issues on its agenda changing as the faculty, student body, and core courses change, this group provides a structure for sustaining vitality in the core and evolving a meaningful vision of general education in the university.

A strong general education program does not change with each prevailing pedagogical or political wind, but responds reflectively to various movements and creates its own motion—motion that is needed to energize and sustain broader support for ongoing change in the curriculum.

PART II

———— ■ ————

FORMING AN EVOLVING COMMUNITY BASED UPON A VISION OF GENERAL EDUCATION

This part of the monograph addresses the importance of fostering an academic community around a vision for general education, as was discussed in the first part. It is unwise to regard this process of implementing a program as separate from forming the vision. Strong general education programs build the commitments, constituencies, and tensions of the formative stage into the structures that are formed to implement them.

In identifying principles of good practice for sustaining the vitality of general education programs, we observe the tension between administrative structures and visionary ideals. We have attempted to identify institutional strategies that give life to educational ideals. In doing this, we recognize and applaud the diversity of structures across our institutions and avoid structural prescriptions. Rather, we identify in our principles several features that characterize strong general education programs that may be embodied in a variety of organizational structures.

Principle #7:
Strong General Education Programs Require and Foster Academic Community.

The successful incorporation of vision into practice depends on the ability of program designers to create the conditions for community. The importance of creating and sustaining community has a solid empirical base. Alexander Astin (1993) assessed a broad range of features associated with general education programs and concluded, "The student's peer group is the single most potent source of influence on growth and development during the undergraduate years" (p. 138). Further, Astin identified faculty-student interaction as the second most powerful influence on undergraduates. Thus, community is not only a feel-good notion; it is empirically related to the educational impact of general education programs.

Although many positive things can be and have been said on behalf of "collegiate community," intellectual isolation, disciplinary fragmentation, and minimal interaction among faculty and students are still facts of life at many American colleges and universities. Viable general education programs work to counteract these alienating forces by creating forums for community. In *The Idea of a University*, John Henry (Cardinal) Newman (1873) asserted that students live together among practitioners of all of the disciplines which, in the university context, come together "to complete, correct, and balance each other" (Discourse V, #1). The opportunity for community is ever present, but it requires special efforts to bridge the fields that are separated by language, administrative structures, and patterns of social interaction.

Development of community—hence, effective outcomes for general education programs—involves relationships in three intertwined dimensions: among students, between faculty and students, and among faculty.

Among Students

Taking the same courses gives students a common experience that builds strong relationships among them. In Astin's words, "...having students take exactly the same general education courses provides a common experience that can stimulate student discussion outside class and facilitate the formation of strong bonds among student peers" (p. 425). Indeed, that is one of the reasons why he found that a "hard core" version of general education, although uncommon, fostered pronounced benefits. Not every institution can or should have this version of general education. But every institution can and should try to build common academic experiences for groups of students that may yield the desirable outcomes associated with core curricula. In strong general education programs, whether based on a core distribution or mixed model, imaginative ways are found to secure the advantages of common academic experiences for students.

Learning communities, for instance, are mechanisms designed to provide community in institutions that are fragmented, whether by large enrollments, student diversity, large numbers of part-time students and faculty, or specialization and curricular divisions. Many institutions are experimenting with learning communities. The state of Washington is leading the nation in these efforts, with over thirty institutions–inspired by exemplary efforts at Seattle Central Community College, North Central Community College, and Skagit Valley Community College–creating learning communities. Many different models for course clustering have been developed that work in different institutional environments. Notable among these are Coordinated Studies (most clearly associated with Evergreen State College), Freshman Interest Groups (at the University of Washington and the University of Oregon) and clusters (with strong models at Laguardia Community College and Western Michigan University).

In the Coordinated Studies Program at The Evergreen State College in Washington, the program, and not the course, is the basic unit of curricular design. Multidisciplinary, theme-oriented programs engage faculty and students full-time for one, two, or three quarters.

In the Freshman Interest Groups Program (FIGS) at the University of Washington, small groups of students share enrollment in related introductory classes that have an overall common theme. Courses are taught in the normal manner with additional meetings and discussions held to tie materials together. Approximately 25 percent of this institution's first year students enroll in this program.

Between Faculty and Students

Community is also fostered through close interactions between faculty and students, both in and outside of the classroom, and within and outside of major programs. Several new pedagogies emphasize active classroom involvement on the part of students and foster close student-faculty work. Collaborative learning, in which students work with peers to complete joint learning tasks, small freshman or senior seminars, or courses focusing on the development of writing and other skills, are examples. The key is for faculty-student relationships to be close enough for each to observe the other's thinking processes—and to respond to each other's thoughts. Realizing that their intellectual dilemmas are shared by their professors empowers students and leads them to become engaged in their studies. And faculty members become better teachers when they not only understand the minds of students but also feel the need to respond to them.

When student-faculty interaction in class is close, it is natural to extend thinking and interaction beyond the classroom. Informal conversations between students and faculty—in laboratories and computer rooms, or even in the snack bar—become a natural extension of conversation begun in the classroom. This social-intellectual interaction is valued so highly by some institutions that they emphasize it from the first day new students set foot on the campus through freshman year programs, often a central part of general education. It is no accident that such programs have been found to increase freshman satisfaction, achievement, and retention (Fidler and Hunter, 1989).

The University of Maryland is adding to its 1500 student University Honors Program a whole array of other "living-learning center" programs in which first and second year students live together and pursue a common curriculum of primarily general education courses focused in areas such as international affairs, the performing arts, the life sciences, or science, technology, and society. Four such programs currently exist with more planned for the future.

Among Faculty

Interactions among faculty across disciplinary lines, whether in interdisciplinary curricular projects, shared faculty development initiatives, or simply conversations about intellectual issues are essential to sustain, as well as to initiate, a sense of community. Across all of the campuses involved in this project, participants noted the enormous good will and energy generated by simple and often inexpensive ways to foster conversations and interactions among faculty. Scheduling retreats, workshops, or conversation hours; buying copies of a book to encourage faculty members' participation in a seminar or discussion series; or providing lunch for a group of faculty members gathered together for conversation on an issue of common interest: all foster a sense of community.

Strong general education programs involve team planning—not necessarily team teaching—by groups of faculty members. Selecting texts for a world literature course, developing a syllabus for a freshman seminar, or revising guidelines for a mathematics requirement: all involve faculty members working together. These group activities lead individuals to move beyond reference to "my" student, "my" course, and "my" department to a broader sense of communal responsibility and ownership of "our" students and "our" curriculum. They generate—and regenerate—a sense of shared educational purpose.

The experience of Roanoke College testifies to the rich results that can come from team work. From the beginning of their general education program, course design was a group effort, the work of faculty who would be teaching in each course. Lists of core works and topics, guidelines which shape all sections, the critical thinking goals of the course: all have been designed and revised by the faculty involved, working as a group.

These are some of the reasons why Larry Goodwin, Academic Vice President, observes, "At The College of St. Scholastica, the reform of the general education program has been an exercise in community building."

COMMUNITY AND THE ST. JOSEPH'S COLLEGE CORE

An eight-semester, forty-five-credit-hour, team-taught core curriculum has been in place for twenty-five years, One of the principal motives of the original designers was the formation of genuine academic community. It was inspired both by Newman's idea of the university as a place where students "live among practitioners of all the disciplines" and by the stress on community in the Second Vatican Council. This goal has been achieved over the ensuing years, largely because the Core Curriculum was implemented with design features that deliberately worked at institutionalizing community-building activities.

Student-to-student relationships are different from those at other colleges, primarily because *all* of the full-time students have a common academic experience. No matter what their major, all students have this common intellectual fund—books, lectures, assignments—as "community property" throughout all four years. Students attest to the impact that this experience has on conversations in the dining hall and residence halls. There is an unusual degree of "class identity" (e.g., freshman, senior) at Commencement and alumni/ae gatherings–and it is of a distinctly academic nature.

Because professors running the discussion sections in Core have to work, more frequently than not, with readings and lectures that come from outside their field of specialization, there is a peculiarly different relationship between faculty and students in Core. The professor is not in the classroom as someone lecturing within the confines of his/her discipline but rather as an "advanced" or "master" learner along with students. This not only favors the use of more collaborative and active pedagogical styles in the Core discussions, but also puts the professor in the role of a "lifelong learner." It models the kind of person that the College aims to encourage in each of its graduates.

Because every one of the segments of Core designed by a team of faculty members from several departments, faculty-to-faculty relationships have been greatly modified. Professors in other departments are not aliens, much less competitors, but true colleagues. They know one another, they dialogue and debate with each other, and they share common commitment to the growth and development of the same students.

Principle #8:
Strong General Education Programs Have
Strong Faculty and Administrative Leadership.

The organization chart of a college or university is a good indicator of the seriousness of purpose about general education at that institution. A strong general education program will not be housed in a "spare room." It will have a specific administrator in charge of the program and often others responsible for its major components (e.g. a director of writing or first year seminars); an academic committee to provide oversight and direction; clearly established lines of authority, responsibility, and accountability for the curriculum; and its own budget.

Although the chief academic officer is formally responsible for the entire academic program, that individual has too many responsibilities to provide day-to-day leadership for general education. When general education was thought of as simply exposure to a breadth of disciplines, and students selected their own courses from among a large menu, little central coordination was needed. But if the curriculum is designed to cultivate specific knowledge and skills among all students, and if we aspire to curricular coherence, greater coordination is essential. That is why many institutions with new curricula designate an administrator to be solely or primarily responsible for general education. Whether called a director, coordinator, dean, or associate dean of general studies, these new positions—aided by a general education committee—provide systematic oversight and planning.

ADMINISTRATORS OF
GENERAL EDUCATION PROGRAMS

During the October 1991 meetings of the Association for General and Liberal Studies, nineteen participants, all of whom held some administrative responsibility for general/ liberal education programs in their respective institutions, attended a session scheduled for "General Education Directors." The participants agreed that an organization of general education administrators would be desirable, primarily to share ideas and provide information. This group also suggested that attempts be made to schedule similar sessions for program administrators at the national meetings of the Association of American Colleges and the American Association for Higher Education.

Subsequent meetings have resulted in the development of a list of 127 program administrators. Thirty percent of this group hold the title "director"; 23 percent are "deans"—half of these administer general education as a primary responsibility, and the other half have administration of general education as one of several programmatic responsibilities; 12 percent are "associate" or "assistant deans"; 16 percent are "coordinators"; 12 percent are "chairpersons"; and 6 percent are "associate" or "assistant provosts." Forty percent of these administrators are located in liberal arts colleges, 52 percent are in state universities, 7 percent are in research institutions, and 3 are from community colleges.

These administrators indicate a considerable range of time is devoted to their general education responsibilities. Several deans, for example, consider general education program administration as a primary responsibility, requiring nearly full-time on the various tasks, while other deans devote time to general education administration as one of many responsibilities. Directors and coordinators generally receive some release time during all or part of the academic year, and a few individuals function as full-time faculty members, with general education administration considered a service responsibility. For two examples at institutions, see Appendix E.

To sustain vitality in general education, institutions must be every bit as serious about the care of this largest instructional program as for the most important major on campus. The first task of administration is to set institutional priorities, to make clear, firm, and public institutional commitments to the importance of general education. Some would argue that it is nearly impossible to proceed without such rhetorical support by the most prominent institutional leaders. Moreover, these statements must be backed up by actions.

From the faculty point of view, there are three considerations which bring home institutional seriousness of purpose about general education. In *hiring* new faculty, the importance of general education as well as the specialization should be highlighted, and new faculty should be told of expectations that they will contribute both to general education and the academic major. The work that professors do in general education, often the most creative and challenging kind of teaching, should count significantly in *promotion and tenure* decisions. In these decisions, pedagogical scholarship and interdisciplinary research must be recognized in the same way, with equal weight as traditional discipline-based scholarship. The same point needs to be made when *funding* is allocated for salary increments and awards are made for faculty development projects. Without clear evidence of commitment in these tangible ways, few faculty members will devote themselves to keeping general education vital.

In colleges and universities organized by departments built around academic disciplines, a tension between loyalties to the specialty and general education is built in. Sometimes the disciplinary major and general education are seen to be in opposition. But as Ernest Boyer (1987, 290) observes, "Rather than divide the undergraduate experience into separate camps—general versus specialized education—the curriculum of a college of quality will bring the two together."

Relationships between general education and academic majors are points of ongoing negotiation. In order to be strong, general education programs must sustain intense feelings of ownership by faculty who are rooted in disciplines, offering them opportunities to transcend specific disciplinary limits. A balance must be struck between departmental and institutional priorities, so that students may benefit from *both* strong academic majors and strong general education curricula.

INVENTORY OF INSTITUTIONAL PRACTICES

Two academics from the University of Minnesota-Morris sensed the importance of an array of institutional policies and procedures that affect the operation of the core curriculum. Mary Ruth Cox, Assistant Dean, and Peter Whelan, Assistant Professor of Geology, developed an inventory to identify factors that help or hinder the curriculum.

The "Inventory of Supports for General Education Programs in Undergraduate Institutions" contain items in the following categories:

1. Faculty recruitment, hiring, and orientation
2. Faculty promotion, tenure, and merit awards
3. Coherence between general education and the major
4. Governance support for general education
5. Assessment of general education
6. Student affairs support for general education
7. Ongoing institutional support for general education, and
8. Promotional and public relations support for general education.

This is a useful device to heighten awareness, generate discussion, and, ultimately, develop policies that deliberately support the core curriculum. Copies of the Inventory are available in *Talking Points*, a publication of AAC.

Principle #9:
Strong General Education Programs Cultivate Substantial and Enduring Support from Multiple Constituencies.

The operational concept of general education is a collective one; it comes from the independent and collaborative efforts of faculty members, administrators, students, and external constituencies. These various groups have changing memberships that represent diverse and sometimes conflicting perceptions and interests. As these groups work together to develop and articulate their understandings of general education, they can sustain program integrity, relevance, and vitality by remaining focused on educational first principles. The necessary program-wide efforts to assess and restate commitments, to foster creativity in course design and teaching, to respond meaningfully to institutional and societal change depend on such focus and collaboration.

Engaging many constituencies in developing an institutional vision for general education poses great challenges. Generating feelings of program ownership among the whole faculty is central to the task. A strong general education program also needs the support of academic and other administrators. Their decisions can center institutional priorities on the essential purposes of undergraduate education.

Administrators also can exercise influence with constituencies so that they highlight the centrality of general education.

Students who understand the role and purpose of general education and are committed to it are its best ambassadors. Working with peers, faculty, and administrators, students can gain a deeper sense of the purpose and values of the program, as well as a sense of its benefits for their futures.

After a humanities class, one Ball State honors student said, "My biggest fear in life is to graduate, get a job in my field, and never, ever again have a conversation like the ones we have in this class." Isn't this what we want students to feel when they leave our General Studies courses?

One university managed to implement a comprehensive new general education curriculum in the face of vocal opposition from a minority of the faculty. At an open forum the naysayers appeared "loaded for bear." They argued, as they had from the outset, that the program was ill-conceived, imposed too many demands on majors, and had little support. Then students spoke. They spoke eloquently from their own experience about having learned to think and to write clearly, having gained many more important perspectives on the world, having come to appreciate the contributions of many disciplines, and to achieve a greater understanding of themselves. Several voiced the view that it was the best part of their education. These personal statements grounded in their own experiences were welcomed by the faculty. They gave valuable support to the defenders of the curriculum at a critical time in its history.

THE LIBERAL ARTS INSTITUTE
AT ROANOKE COLLEGE

At Roanoke College the Liberal Arts Institute has been crafted to give staff and faculty a clear understanding of the purpose and content of Roanoke's new general education curriculum which they can then communicate to students,

parents, staff, faculty and members of the surrounding
community as they go about their daily work.

In a series of twelve three-hour meetings taking place
over a three week span in the summer, and monthly during
the academic year, faculty from the different general
education courses introduce their courses: explaining their
purposes and teaching a typical class. Staff from
Admissions, Public Relations, Resource Development,
Student Affairs, together with faculty not teaching in the
new curriculum, are among the participants.

The intention of the Institute is that every member of
the faculty and staff be able to serve as a spokesperson for
the new general education curriculum: answering questions, meeting criticisms, and speaking with enthusiasm for
the program.

Off-campus constituencies also can serve the purposes of general
education.

After developing a distinctive new core curriculum, one
private university wrote to all the high school counselors
in its region to describe the changes. It also invited
counselors from the local metropolitan region to campus
for a luncheon briefing on the new curriculum. Both drew
generous praise for the higher expectations and greater
structure of the program. It is not accidental that freshman
enrollment spurted 33 percent the next two years.

Parents, too, can be enlisted to the cause.

During its summer orientation sessions for new students at
Southeast Missouri State University, a separate session is
held for parents. They are asked to write down what they
would most like their children to learn. When the results
are compared, they invariably are close to the goals of the
curriculum. Parents then are shown how the curriculum is
designed to address those purposes. "This always generates
a lot of commitment to the curriculum and long-term

support for what our students study," reports John Hinni, Dean of the School of University Studies.

Employers and alumni, too, are sometimes consulted. Some institutions survey employers and alumni about the qualities that are desired in graduates. Typically the result is a profile that reflects a broad, general education, e.g., the abilities to think clearly and critically, to express themselves well, to work independently as well as in a group, to get along with diverse people. Corporate leaders and alumni frequently serve on boards of trustees, who themselves can be an important constituency. Two faculty members (Ford and Sheridan, 1992, 30) argued that "Trustees can serve as a window to the world for faculty. Boards are uniquely qualified to ask some helpful questions, such as: How well are our students served by our curriculum? Are proposed changes designed to better educate our current students or to attract different ones? What are the costs and benefits of proposed changes? How does the curriculum reflect our mission and heritage?"

Promoting feelings of joint ownership of general education across diverse constituencies is a delicate balancing act. A sustained process of discussion, debate, and definition is needed to produce a collective vision firmly grounded in the culture of the institution. Indeed, this process itself is a critical element in building and maintaining strong foundations for general education.

ADVISORY COUNCIL FOR THE LIBERAL ARTS

The College of Letters and Science at the University of Idaho has an Advisory Council. Consisting of alumni and community leaders, it works with the Dean on a variety of projects to advance the interests of liberal education. In the recent past it has given assistance to graduates seeking jobs, advice about raising the stature of the College of Letters and Science within the University, and counsel to faculty members and administrators about curriculum ideas. Community advisory councils are common in professional schools, and this represents a successful attempt to enlist support from community leaders for the liberal arts and sciences.

NEW JERSEY ADVISORY COUNCIL
ON GENERAL EDUCATION

The New Jersey Board of Higher Education appointed a remarkable collection of corporate and academic leaders to an Advisory Council on General Education. It concluded (1990, 29): "...a substantial convergence has emerged between the academic and economic communities, both for their growing concern about general education and in their definition of those aspects of general education which deserve emphasis at this time. Because this convergence has taken place around goals that have always been highly valued in the academy (e.g., critical thinking, clear expression of ideas), we believe it constitutes a major opportunity to reinvigorate general education in accordance with these traditional academic values—but now with the support of the economic community and with a strengthened hand in speaking credibly to even career-oriented students."

Principle #10:
Strong General Education Programs Ensure Continuing Support for Faculty, Especially as They Engage in Dialogues Across Academic Specialties

Faculty commitments and capabilities make or break the implementation of curriculum change, and they are central to sustaining program vitality. Faculty design and teach the courses and instruct the students: they are a program's most important resource. That is why strong general education programs continuously provide faculty support. Some institutions have been successful at securing extramural support for such faculty development activities.

Saint Joseph's College has aggressively pursued faculty development funds from private and federal sources for about twenty years. That activity has funded a continuing plan for curriculum and faculty development projects related to the core curriculum such as integrated science segments, intercultural core components, and interdisciplinary teaching skills.

At Grand Valley State University, the National Science Foundation is supporting the development of a new multicultural mathematics course which is intended as a general education offering in a category called formal and quantitative reasoning. The grant is supporting an interdisciplinary team including mathematicians, computer scientists, an engineer, anthropologist, an urban planner, and a sociologist to construct a course which uses the dwelling places of various groups as a vehicle to teach geometry and to promote multicultural understanding and knowledge.

At Fort Lewis College in Colorado, the National Endowment for the Humanities is supporting the development of a new Human Heritage course for their general education curriculum. The course focuses on the peoples of European origin, the peoples native to the Americas, and the people of China. Summer faculty development workshops have enabled faculty from diverse disciplinary perspectives to work together in developing this new offering.

When a new curriculum is implemented, faculty need support to learn new content and new approaches to teaching and learning. If general education involves courses on world history, writing-intensive courses, interdisciplinary core courses, or senior seminars, for example, these are new to many faculty members. They may need to learn new subject matter that allows them to reach beyond their familiar specializations. Similarly, a biologist and a sociologist, for instance, may need help in teaching writing, e.g., devising writing assignments, assessing written work, and giving constructive feedback to students. In our experience large numbers of faculty members are eager to participate in seminars and workshops to broaden areas of expertise or learn new teaching approaches, if they are given proper support.

Although it is important for faculty to see continuous improvement of the curriculum as part of their day-to-day work in the profession, additional support for substantially new curricular initiatives is necessary to ensure successful implementation of major reforms. It is not unusual for a small college to develop one hundred new or significantly revised courses, if it makes a dramatic change. Large institutions often do more. Often courses of a certain type must be planned, at least in part, by a team to assure that all courses or sections address common goals or follow certain guidelines. It takes time for faculty members to hammer out common understandings and to reach agreement about topics, concepts, texts, and examinations.

After a curriculum is successfully implemented, some people tend to assume that the program can be put on cruise control, that it can run itself. That is a mistake. A small cadre of professors may, indeed, be teaching a first year seminar or a values component, but some will go on leave, others will take another position, and still others will decide to move on to other interests. New individuals must continually be brought into the program, presenting an ongoing challenge to socialize the newcomers and to incorporate the new perspectives into the program. Ten years after one university adopted a new core, half of its faculty had changed. The newcomers found themselves teaching in a curriculum they neither understood nor felt was theirs.

Even veterans of curricular revisions need to be refreshed and reminded of curricular commitments.

> Thomas Lowe, Director of General Studies and Academic Programs at Ball State University, conducted a workshop for senior faculty, all of whom had been through a 1985 revision. He observed, "...it is amazing how little they knew, or how much they had forgotten, about the program and the role of general studies on our campus. [We] should not assume the notices, memos, newsletters [we] send out do very much to inform busy faculty about general education. Something beyond the traditional modes of communication is called for."

Interdisciplinary teaching and learning, especially, cannot take place without ongoing discussions among the faculty. Integrating materials, reshaping a course, and connecting with one another's disciplines take time and energy. Although these must all be supported, they don't always require large stipends.

What is in it for faculty members to learn new material, make intellectual connections with other disciplines, or work with colleagues to refine courses? A great deal that can be summarized as professional and personal renewal results from such activities. We have heard from many faculty members who have talked of new insights, a burst of energy, renewed enthusiasm for teaching, enrichment from considering new perspectives, and satisfaction from teaching non-majors. In fact, the process of developing and refining curricula may well be the very best form of professional development for professors.

Faculty members become enthusiastic supporters of general education insofar as they see their involvement in such programs as providing opportunities for them to take new perspectives on their work in their disciplines, to discover connections with the work of colleagues in other disciplines, or to explore new approaches to teaching and learning that enhance their effectiveness in working with students.

Correlates of Faculty Development

Leaders at campuses making changes in their general education curricula attest to the importance of continuing attention to the development of the faculty involved in teaching the core. A survey of 226 diverse colleges and universities solicited information about the changes they made and their associated consequences. The following table contains the reported outcomes according to whether the institution had "no systematic program" or "a major program" of faculty development to implement their changes. As the table summarizes, significant attention to the development of faculty was associated with more favorable attitudes toward general education; reported increases in program quality, coherence, and similar dimensions; and positive impacts on various aspects of institutional functioning. And faculty gained a good deal of professional renewal.

	FACULTY DEVELOPMENT	
	No Program	Major Program
Attitudes toward General Education more favorable:		
Administrators	52	84
Faculty	49	83
Students	21	51
Quite a lot or very much change in:		
Faculty renewal	23	89
Higher-quality education	40	82
Greater curricular coherence	38	77
More active learning	24	68
Revitalized institution	27	68
Greater appreciation for diversity	35	55
Positive impact on:		
Faculty renewal	48	88
Institutional identity	58	87
Sense of community	51	79
Public relations	48	75
Efficient utilization of faculty	36	65
Admissions	21	65
General education budget	32	62
Retention	24	58
Fund raising	20	57
Faculty reward structure	12	42

Source: *New Life for the College Curriculum*, Jerry G. Gaff, 1991

Principle #11:
Strong General Education Programs Reach Beyond the Classroom to the Broad Range of Student Co-curricular Experiences.

Most general education programs try to provide an integrative focus for students' undergraduate experience, linking seemingly disparate parts of the curriculum into a larger whole. However, in reality, such attempts at forging connections may function as artificial and superfluous impositions if they are not based in an understanding of the lives of students. The contexts for students' meaning-making extend well beyond the walls of our classrooms.

General education programs strive to tear down some of the walls between disciplines, opening new doors or windows in the classroom walls dividing philosophy and political science or sociology and zoology. However, the even more formidable walls separating students' experience of the curriculum from other components of their daily lives are strong countervailing forces to the best of these integrative efforts. Students see connections and ask questions about meaning and value in the curriculum insofar as these intellectual habits or dispositions are encouraged by their involvements outside as well as inside of the classroom.

The desired reach of most general education programs is indeed broad. As noted in earlier sections of this document, claims are made that far exceed mastery of fixed content or development of specified skills. Rather, more ambitious and idealistic goals like training for citizenship, broadening intellectual perspectives, or influencing values and ethical decision-making often are envisioned. Yet the reach of even the most ambitious of the courses in our formal curricula is quite restricted by comparison.

How, then, can general education programs—representing typically 30–50 percent of the formal curriculum—close the gap between lofty program aspirations and their limited role in the formal curriculum? One way is to harness the power of co-curricular factors to serve the educational purposes of the curriculum.

Student learning occurs in residence halls, employment settings, commuter car pools, dining halls, on the athletic field, in extracurricular activities, volunteer community service projects, in the laundry room, and the hallways outside classes. However, the approaches of many general education programs do little to capitalize on the extraordinary resources for learning that already exist in the varied activities in the daily lives of students.

Connected learning calls for actively making relationships
between fields, applying knowledge from one context to
another, and taking seriously students' interests in relating
academic learning to the wider world of public issues as
well as individual experiences and goals.
—*The Challenge of Connecting Learning*, Association of
American Colleges, 1991, p.19.

Those studying the impact of college on students (Feldman and
Newcomb, 1969, Pascarella and Terenzini 1991), have documented
the vast array of influences on students beyond the formal curriculum.
Astin (1993) specifically highlights the relationships between a number
of non-curricular experiences for students and a wide variety of
quantitative indices of the success of general education programs.

Michael Moffatt's ethnography, *Coming of Age in New Jersey*
(1978), suggests that much of what students learn in colleges or universities comes from sources other than their classroom encounters
with faculty and assigned texts.

Strong working relationships between general education programs
and staff involved in student affairs provide a natural venue for consistent integration of the curriculum and co-curriculum (Knefelkamp,
1984). Yet, the mistrust and lack of understanding between Student
Affairs and Academic Affairs on many campuses is difficult to overcome. Each has its own mission and agenda for students, and rarely do
the two meet, except on the organization chart. Because faculty view
themselves as concerned primarily with the intellectual domain and
student affairs personnel are primarily concerned with the affective
and social domains, the two seldom find common ground for programming. Ironically, we ask our students to take on integrative tasks, to
develop multiple ways of thinking and knowing, but often refuse to do
so ourselves.

Programming that allows students to take the academic discourse
of the classroom into the community is particularly beneficial. Far too
many students sit in classes semester after semester convinced that
what goes on in the classroom has little to do with "real life." By forg-

ing connections between the texts of the classroom and the "texts" outside the classroom walls, strong general education programs help students make connections about who they are, what they think, and how they act.

At the University of Hartford, the general education course on epidemics and AIDS has been very successful in integrating out-of-classroom experiences. Students in this course are required to participate in a health campaign that takes place both on- and off-campus. Guest speakers are invited into the residence halls; student-to-student teaching and work off campus are parts of the out-of-class learning. The students from Hartt School of Music who are enrolled in this course often perform in a hospice as part of their out-of-class work; art students have auctioned art work to raise money for an AIDS hospice.

Other interesting examples of attempts to coordinate out of classroom experiences with the curriculum certainly exist, including internships, field observations and community service projects. However, most institutions have barely scratched the surface in the search for ways to extend student learning beyond the walls of the classroom. Examples are found for a few courses in the curriculum at many institutions, but broader curriculum-wide emphases on integrating out-of-classroom experiences are indeed rare.

It is also the case that the most successful of these efforts to integrate out-of-classroom experiences target eighteen to twenty-two year-old full-time students in residential college environments—a minority of those enrolled in higher education today. A distinct challenge to most general education programs at this time is to reconceive the co-curriculum in the broadest possible sense; to ask questions about maximizing the utility of general education as a meaningful frame of reference for organizing the varied lives of the diverse students on our campuses.

Radical redefinitions of teaching and learning may recognize the complexity and variety of influences on students' lives beyond the classroom. Attempting to insulate the curriculum from the competing demands of work, family, church, and community will meet with minimal success.

A better approach is to encourage students to reflect on their experiences and understand the power of general education for making meaning of the materials of their daily lives.

Principle #12:
Strong General Education Programs Assess and Monitor Progress Toward an Evolving Vision Through Ongoing Self-Reflection

We view assessment as part of a continuous process of program development in strong general education programs. Assessment of course and program impact through a variety of methods results in more effective pedagogy, better courses, and more refined conceptions of requirements. In conceiving of general education as a lively intellectual project, faculty bring their natural curiosity and scholarly dispositions to their teaching and curricular design efforts.

Most of our general education programs have institutionalized assessment in some fashion. Some programs routinely administer standardized tests. Others are using locally designed instruments, student interviews, focus groups, or surveys of current students or alumni/ae. Still others are using portfolio-based approaches to assessment. Thus, various data that might facilitate self-reflection and evaluation are often collected. However, examples of the systematic use of such data in ongoing deliberations about the curriculum are much more difficult to identify.

Systematic use of assessment data is exactly what we advocate. Assessment is not a superfluous activity, nor is it primarily for the benefit of external agencies. Government, foundations, or accreditation agencies may require reports for their various purposes. However, we see assessment as the absolutely vital implementation link between the evolving general education program (Principle 6) and the purposes it is to achieve as specified by "the point" of the program and its role in the mission of the institution (Principles 1 and 2).

This contrasts with what often is an episodic approach to curriculum implementation. Too often goal statements for general education programs are the subject of intense debate, and initial design of curricula to meet these goals may involve faculty actively for limited periods of time. In this sense, general education curricula have often functioned as finished products, wrapped and hermetically sealed after periods of intensely involving debate and opened on a cyclical basis every ten years or so with trepidation and hesitation. Thus the general education "package" can be put on the shelf for a while, and faculty can turn their energies to the daily demands of teaching and research. Courses are modified, added and deleted in a kind of routinized bureaucratic exercise, with not much attention by anyone to the drift from original program intentions.

Strong general education programs, on the other hand, involve faculty oversight groups in ongoing review of questions about teaching and learning; they include the perspectives of faculty, students, and external constituencies. Assessment of program effectiveness is particularly challenging because of the complex agenda of general education programs. Answers may be sought from the rich array of data gathered throughout the year.

At American University and Miami University syllabi for all sections of all general education offerings are collected each semester. Oversight committees review these syllabi to monitor drift of courses from original intentions as well as evolution in desired directions.

Arizona State University has initiated a long-term panel study of a representative sample of undergraduate students. The purpose of this is to understand better the dynamics surrounding an undergraduate education and the particular role general studies plays in this process. Approximately 1,000 students are participating in this six-year project. Part of this study is focusing on the in- and out-of-class impact of taking general studies courses. Data are being collected through a variety of means, including focus groups, telephone and mail surveys, interviews, and transcript analysis.

Moreover, we need to develop a larger view of students and a more complete understanding of their experiences in the curriculum. Strong general education programs seek evidence of the effectiveness of their programs in meeting stated objectives by attending carefully to the intersection of student learning with program goals.

At Susquehanna University thirteen students enrolled in a Core Evaluation Class in which they read and discussed both literature on general education and university-generated documents on the core at their own institution. They then divided into four teams to examine different aspects of the core, collected appropriate syllabi and interviewed faculty. Their findings constituted a report and recommendations to the curriculum committee.

At Union College twenty-five student volunteers participated in a "Student assessment Project" for General Education. They met weekly for dinner and ongoing discussion of the function of general education to enhance their intellectual awareness and to collect assessment materials on the program. During one term, they interviewed over 150 of their peers, talked with faculty and administrators, and compiled their results. In the following term, they presented their findings through panels, reports, and papers to students, faculty, and administrators. Student response to this project has been positive.

To assess is thus to judge the fulfillment of promises, the achievement of hopes, in an evolving and purposeful process. Strong general education programs use assessment data in a systematic, ongoing, process of continuous improvement of the curriculum.

CONCLUSION

As noted in describing and exemplifying each of the principles in this document, strong general education programs resist classification as a simple polar opposite to study in the disciplines. Strong general education programs are not conveniently labeled as beginning work, in contrast to advanced work; as general work, in contrast to specialized work; nor as theoretical work, in contrast to practical or applied work. Rather, strong general education programs challenge the boundaries and structures of traditional knowledge claims within the university.

Strong general education programs are, consequently, sources of disequilibrium within their institutions. In fact, such programs are inherently transformative: students gain both a broadened context and the methodologies whereby they may interrogate the disciplines and thereby shape their relationships to knowledge.

Strong general education programs are similarly transformative in affording faculty opportunities to transcend narrow disciplinary loyalties in the pursuit of common goals. Common purposes and goals are forged through ongoing and sometimes difficult discussions among colleagues across disciplines. What is achieved defines institutional character.

Strong general education programs advocate an ecological approach to resource allocation and planning. The zero-sum game of financing higher education has often placed general education in opposition to study in the disciplines in the fight for student credit hours and resource allocations. Strong general education programs challenge that opposition, realizing that the quality of disciplinary programs thrives in the nutritive medium they provide.

In studying the undergraduate major, an earlier AAC report (1991) noted the important function of the major as the disciplinary *home* within the college or university. Extending this metaphor, strong general education programs provide the *neighborhood* for these homes in the disciplines—each neighborhood having a distinct character, local customs, and established patterns of interaction. Financial advisors caution that one is far better served by buying the cheapest home in a good neighborhood than the most expensive and lavish home in a bad neighborhood. Likewise, building a lavish disciplinary home in a poor general education environment is not a wise investment.

Institution-wide dialogues based in critical self-examination and reflection are a major source of renewal and change in colleges and universities. The prologue to this essay outlines the foci of today's dialogues on college campuses. Faculties on campus after campus are concluding that strong general education programs are needed if we are to have an informed citizenry in a complex, pluralistic society nearing the end of the twentieth century.

Strong general education programs emphasize the value of teaching. They cultivate teaching and learning strategies that draw from and emphasize multiple ways of knowing. They encourage the development of strategies which illuminate the connectedness of knowledge and of the disciplines, rather than their fragmentation. They connect in- and out-of-classroom experiences.

This booklet would be deficient, if, after arguing for the aim of connecting knowledge, it did not point out some of the connections between and among its twelve principles. Although the twelve principles were discovered inductively, they do not constitute a mere list of points about good practice; they are an interconnected set of mutually reinforcing propositions. And they are presented in a deliberate order in this publication.

The complementary relationship of Part I and Part II, of articulating and implementing the vision for general education, has already been discussed. But there is also a meaningful order to the six principles within each part. The first two pairs of principles (#1 and #2; #7 and #8) are *foundational*, in that they articulate, on the one hand, the vision of what the general education program for each particular institution is intended to be, and they assign, on the other hand, the responsibility for the conduct of the program to the whole faculty and the whole administration.

The next three principles in each part (#3, #4, and #5; #9, #10, and #11) deal with what is *distinctive* about general education in comparison with other programs at the institution. The vision that provides identity for general education distinguishes it from any academic major in the institution, in that general education seeks coherence among the various ways of knowing, acknowledges its value commitments and moral-political involvements, and makes use of all the richness to be found in the lived experience of students. In regard to implementation, the distinctive aspects are the wide-ranging support that is required from all parts of the academic community to fulfill the purposes of strong general education, the new role that faculty accept in working to develop their own integrative skills, and the use of outside-the-classroom experiences at the service of student growth and development.

Finally, the last principle in each part (#6; #12) is the *dynamic* element. Since students grow, society changes, and faculty refine their vision, general education programs evolve; and the implementation strategy that directs this evolution along the right paths is assessment. Thus we come full circle, in that the last principle directs our attention back to the first, the point of general education.

At this time, over a decade and a half into its third revival this century, general education has come of age. Along with other leaders of American higher education, we know that general education is both a rich concept and a continuing ideal. We know why it is important to the education of students; we have numerous examples of good practice in all kinds of colleges and universities; we know how to conduct a curriculum review and to orchestrate revisions. Moreover, we know what it takes to implement a design once it is approved. Now we have a set of principles for sustaining vitality in operational programs, for giving expression to the ideals of general education in institutional settings.

What remains to be done is for each college or university to utilize what has been learned by a generation of curriculum reformers to provide strong foundations for the general education component of its baccalaureate degree programs. An effective broad general education for all students is a goal that is within our reach.

APPENDICES

APPENDIX A

ARIZONA

Articulation agreements exist between the three Arizona state universities (Arizona State University, the University of Arizona, and Northern Arizona University) and the Arizona community colleges. These agreements relate to the applicability of transfer credit from a community college to a four year institution in the state of Arizona. Arizona has the second largest community college system in the United States. These various articulation agreements greatly aid in the transition of a student from one institution to another.

In addition to the establishment of articulation agreements, the Arizona public community colleges and universities have agreed upon a common structure for a general education core curriculum. This core curriculum provides students attending any Arizona public, postsecondary institution with the opportunity to build a core general education program which is transferable to any other state institution without loss of credit. This common agreement is called the Transfer General Education Core Curriculum (TGECC). The TGECC is transferable from one Arizona community college to another. Students transferring from an Arizona community college to one of the three state universities have the option of completing the lower division general education requirements at the university to which they transfer or completing the TGECC.

CALIFORNIA

In California, both the University of California (UC) and California State University (CSU) have multiple campuses which serve both native students (beginning as freshmen) and transfer students primarily from community colleges. UC campuses have complete autonomy while the CSU general education requirements are mandated in the state education code. While the two systems draw from different student populations, have different teaching loads for faculty, grant different degrees, and have different funding bases, they all face the dilemma of providing a balanced, integrated program to all students, no matter where the student begins his/her college education. To this end, a statewide intersegmental committee (composed of community colleges, UC, and CSU faculty) designed and implemented a common transfer curriculum that is accepted by all public universities and satisfies 75 percent of the state general education requirements.

MINNESOTA

Missions change, sometimes rather abruptly, especially in a climate of fiscal constraint. Consider the changing relationships among the public-sector institutions in Minnesota. The University of Minnesota struck a deal with the state's political leaders to reduce the number of its freshman and sophomore students by over 5000, to keep the amount of state support level, and to use additional funds to improve quality by increasing course sections, reducing class size, and improving advising for undergraduates. The Twin Cities campus, the state's flagship campus, also developed a comprehensive university-wide core curriculum presided over by a revived Council of Liberal Education. In a parallel action, the Minnesota State University (a separate system from the University of Minnesota) recently decided to cap its enrollment because its financial support was insufficient to support quality. Both of these systems are relying more on community colleges to give undergraduates a high quality general education. As a result, the academic transfer mission is becoming more important at Minnesota community colleges. Responding to a legislative mandate to improve the ease of transfer, the three systems, along with the technical colleges, have worked together to develop a transfer curriculum. Far more than articulation agreements, this course of study is collaboratively designed and implemented by groups of faculty members from all disciplines and campuses. The new structure at the University has made it possible for the other systems to adapt their programs to it. Although the basic missions of each sector remain, the fact is that each promotes increased quality in undergraduate general education.

APPENDIX B

MISSISSIPPI

Jackson State University has a distinguished history, rich in the tradition of educating young men and women for leadership, having undergone seven name changes as it grew and developed. Founded as Natchez Seminary in 1877 by the American Baptist Home Mission Society, the school was established at Natchez, Mississippi, "for the moral, religious and intellectual improvement of Christian leaders of the colored people of Mississippi and the neighboring states." In November 1882, the school was moved to Jackson; in March 1899, the curriculum was expanded and the name was changed to Jackson College. The state assumed support of the college in 1940, assigning to it the mission of training teachers. Subsequently, between 1953 and 1956, the curriculum was expanded to include a graduate program and bachelor's programs in the arts and sciences; the name was changed to Jackson State College in 1956. Further expansion of the curriculum and a notable building program preceded the elevation of Jackson State College to university status on March 15, 1974. In 1979, Jackson State was officially designated the Urban University of the State of Mississippi.

Its special commission to serve as the Urban University is being pursued through programs and activities which seek solutions for urban problems.

Jackson State University seeks to develop persons who can and will assume prominent roles in the dynamics of societal growth and change. For this purpose, resources of the University are applied to the discovery, transmittal, and preservation of knowledge. The University is pledged to the advancement of a free society and the continued progress of democracy. The major task of the University is to guide students in acquiring the knowledge and developing the skills, understandings, appreciations, and attitudes which are essential to general, liberal, and professional education. Situations and activities are designed to prepare students to choose learning experiences, to initiate careers, and to contribute to the social, cultural, and economic development of the state, nation and world.

As in the past, many of our students will continue to come from low income families and bring with them associated cultural, social and academic disadvantages which need special attention. However, as Jackson State develops its mission as a major urban university, special efforts will continually be made to attract academically gifted and nontraditional students in order to maintain and expand the cosmopolitan nature of the student body.

APPENDIX C

SAN JOSE STATE UNIVERSITY

At San Jose State University (SJSU) the strongest commitment to social responsibility is seen in the Cultural Pluralism requirement which has evolved over the past 13 years and continues to evolve. One of the primary general education goals at SJSU is to "enhance the ability to live and work intelligently, responsibly, and cooperatively in a multicultural society and in an increasingly interdependent world." In the beginning, faculty were encouraged to address issues of concern to and achievements of women and diverse cultural groups. After a few years, the humanities and social science areas added categories in cross-cultural comparisons and systems. Then a specific Cultural Pluralism requirement was added which focused on a comparison of at least two distinct cultural groups. While the objectives are very clear and widely accepted (to recognize similarities and differences among cultural groups, factors that influence social interaction, cultural influences on behavior, behavior and attitudes of groups different from one's own, factors that influence behavior and attitudes of cultural groups, and application to contemporary social and cultural relations), the course content is not so obvious to everyone. The tension between a relative importance of global awareness of international communities and domestic awareness of ethnic/racial relations continues in discussions of curricular development and reform. Do people become better citizens by understanding the dynamics of their own society or by learning about the world beyond the United States? Currently, SJSU has not chosen one position over the other and is inclusive in its criteria for course certification, recognizing the importance of both an international focus on other societies and a domestic concentration on ethnic and cultural groups in the U.S. However, all courses must focus on the direct interaction of two diverse cultural groups; comparisons of cultures is not enough. Because the requirement must be completed in residence, SJSU is able to maintain high standards set by the campus: that these courses be issue-oriented, include multiple perspectives, and involve students actively in the learning process.

APPENDIX D

GRAND VALLEY STATE UNIVERSITY

At Grand Valley State University in Michigan, the Freshman Seminar is a one-credit Fall semester course which is intended to provide a semester-long orientation to college and particularly to the general education program. Approximately 80 percent of incoming first-year students enroll in this seminar. The course is taught by regular faculty and by staff from student life and from the residence halls. The freshman seminar is preceded by a two-day summer orientation which includes "an academic experience" in which a faculty person introduces students to general education, its relationship to the major and to student activities, and its significance for their academic life.

The seminar provides opportunities for students to assess their individual skills and abilities, and it allows them to have regular contact with a university staff/faculty person outside their major area of study. Students stay with the freshman seminar advisor during their first semester and also during the second semester of their first year, if they have not yet declared a major.

APPENDIX E

SOUTHEAST MISSOURI STATE UNIVERSITY

After devoting seven years to general education revision, Southeast Missouri State University implemented a new program entitled University Studies in the fall of 1988. Simultaneously, Southeast established a School of University Studies with responsibility for the program. In addition to University Studies, the School contains Southeast's Writing Outcomes Program, Honors Program, Governor's Scholars Program, University Museum, and the Center for Scholarship in Teaching and Learning. The Dean of University Studies administers the School, and the University Studies Program is further supported by two half-time administrators: the Coordinator of the Freshman Year Experience Program, since a first-year seminar is a programmatic requirement for all beginning students, and the Director of the Interdisciplinary Program, since nine semester hours of upper-level interdisciplinary courses are also included in the program.

Creating a School, a deanship, and two half-time positions to administer the University Studies Program was very important to the success of the general education revision at Southeast. The action provided the University community with evidence of a high level of institutional, particularly top administrative, commitment and support for general education.

UNIVERSITY OF DENVER

Restructuring of undergraduate studies at the University of Denver occurred following campus-wide discussion of the values and mission of the University. Placing students and learning first while acknowledging that learning takes place in and out of the classroom allowed Denver to implement an administrative structure that acknowledges the institution's goals. The Vice-Provost for Undergraduate Studies has oversight of the core curriculum, honors, academic advising, mentoring, and the Office of Student Life and the Office of Athletics. Eliminating the traditional "turf" battles between student and academic affairs has encouraged greater cooperation and collaboration between the two areas. All major activities related to orientation, retention, undergraduate curricular revision, programming, and coordination are administered from the same office.

In addition, the Vice-Provost works closely with the academic deans to ensure a stronger, more coherent relationship between general education and the majors. As part of the symbolic and working agreement between the divisions and the Vice-Provost's office, the Associate Dean of Arts, Humanities, and Social Sciences and the Associate Dean of Natural Sciences, Mathematics, and Engineering both have dual responsibilities as Associate Deans of Undergraduate Studies. The structure and coordination between and among the various units is designed to foster a "seamless" educational experience for undergraduates.

REFERENCES

Advisory Council on General Education. *Academy, Economy, and Society: Extending and Supporting General Education.* Trenton, NJ: New Jersey Department of Higher Education, 1990.

American Association for the Advancement of Science. *The Liberal Art of Science.* Washington, D.C.: American Association for the Advancement of Science, 1990.

Anderson, M. *Impostors in the Temple.* New York: Simon and Schuster, 1992.

Association of American Colleges. *Integrity in the College Curriculum.* Washington, D.C.: Association of American Colleges, 1985.

Association of American Colleges. *The Challenge of Connecting Learning.* Washington, D.C.: Association of American Colleges, 1991.

Astin, A.W. *What Matters in College?* San Francisco: Jossey-Bass, 1993.

Belenky, M.F., Clinchy, B.M., Goldberger, N.R., and Tarule, J.M. *Women's Ways of Knowing.* New York: Basic Books, 1986.

Bennett, W.J. *To Reclaim a Legacy.* Washington, D.C.: National Endowment for the Humanities, 1984.

Boyer, E.L. *College: The Undergraduate Experience in America.* New York: Harper & Row, 1987.

Boyer, E.L. and Kaplan, M. *Educating for Survival.* New Rochelle, NY: Change Magazine Press, 1977.

Boyer, E.L. and Levine, A. *A Quest for Common Learning.* Washington, D.C.: Carnegie Foundation for the Advancement of Teaching, 1981.

Carnegie Foundation for the Advancement of Teaching. *Missions of the College Curriculum.* San Francisco: Jossey-Bass, 1977.

Carnochan, W. B. *The Battleground of the Curriculum*. Stanford, CA: Stanford University Press, 1993.

Cheney, L.V. *50 Hours: A Core Curriculum for College Students*. Washington, D.C.: National Endowment for the Humanities, 1989.

El-Khawas, E. *Campus Trends, 1987*. Washington, D.C.: American Council on Education, 1987.

El-Khawas, E. *Campus Trends, 1988*. Washington, D.C.: American Council on Education, 1988.

Elbow, P., *What Is English?*. New York: Modern Language Association of American; Urbana, IL: Council of Teachers of English, 1990.

Erickson, B.L. and Strommer, D.W, *Teaching College Freshmen*. San Francisco: Jossey-Bass, 1991.

Feldman, K.A. and Newcomb, T.M. *The Impact of College on Students*. San Francisco: Jossey-Bass, 1969.

Fidler, P.P. and Hunter, M.S. "How Seminars Enhance Student Success." In M.L. Upcraft and J.N. Gardener (Ed.), *The Freshman Year Experience*. San Francisco: Jossey-Bass, 1989.

Ford, A.T. and Sheridan, J.F. "Moving a Graveyard." *AGB Reports*. May-June, 1992, pp.28-32.

Gaff, J.G. *New Life for the College Curriculum*. San Francisco: Jossey-Bass, 1991.

Gamson, Z.F., "Changing the Meaning of Liberal Education." *Liberal Education*, Nov.-Dec., 1989, pp.10-11.

Graff, G. *Beyond the Culture Wars*. New York: W.W. Norton and Co., 1992.

Hirsch, E.D., Jr. *Cultural Literacy*. Boston: Houghton-Mifflin, 1987.

Johnston, J.S., Jr. and others. "The Demand Side of General Education: Attending to Student Attitudes and Understandings." *Journal of General Education*, Vol. 40, 1991, pp. 180-199.

Kanter, S., London, H., Gamson, Z., Arnold G., and Civian, J. *Subtexts and Garbage Cans; Reforming General Education*. Boston, MA: New England Resource Center for Higher Education, University of Massachusetts at Boston, in press.

Knefelkamp, L.L., *et al.* (eds.) *Applying New Developmental Findings*. New Directions for Student Services, no. 4. San Francisco: Jossey-Bass, 1978.

"Liberal Education at Miami University: A Statement of Principles." In *The Miami Plan for Liberal Education*, Oxford, Ohio: Miami University, 1989.

Moffatt, M., *Coming of Age in New Jersey*. New Brunswick, NJ: Rutgers University Press, 1989.

Musil, C.M., ed. *The Courage to Question: Women's Studies and Student Learning*. Washington, D.C.: Association of American Colleges and National Women's Studies Association, 1992.

Newman, J.H. *The Idea of a University*. New York: Longmans, Green, 1947 (Originally published 1873).

Pascarella, E.T. and Terenzini, P.T. *How College Affects Students*. San Francisco: Jossey-Bass, 1991.

Perry, W.G. *Forms of Intellectual and Ethical Development in the College Years*. New York: Holt, Rinehart & Winston, 1970.

Rudolph, F. *Curriculum: A History of the American Undergraduate Course of Study Since 1636*. San Francisco: Jossey-Bass, 1977.

Schmitz, B. *Core Curriculum and Cultural Pluralism*. Washington, D.C.: Association of American Colleges, 1992.

Schneider, C.S. *The Major As Connected Learning*. New Directions in Higher Education, Jossey-Bass, in press.

Study Group on the Conditions of Excellence in American Higher Education. *Involvement in Learning*. Washington, D.C.: National Institute of Education, 1984.

"Susquehanna University Core Curriculum Handbook." Selinsgrove, PA, n.d.

Task Force on the Core Curriculum. *Report on the Core Curriculum*. Cambridge, MA: Harvard University, 1977.

Task Group on General Education. *New Vitality in General Education*. Washington, D.C.: Association of American Colleges, 1988.

Tinto, V., Goodsell-Love, A., and Russo, P. "Building Community." *Liberal Education*, Fall, 1993, pp.16-21.

Tobias, S. "They're Not Dumb. They're Different." *Change*, July/Aug., 1990, pp. 11-30.

Triesman, P.U., "A Study of the Mathematical Performance of Black Students at the University of California, Berkeley." Berkeley: Mathematics Department, University of California-Berkeley, 1985.